The Big Metric Ninja Foodi Cookbook for UK

1000-Day Ninja Foodi Pressure Cooker and Air Fryer Recipes for Beginners and Advanced Users | With 4 Weeks Meal Plan

Isobel Miles

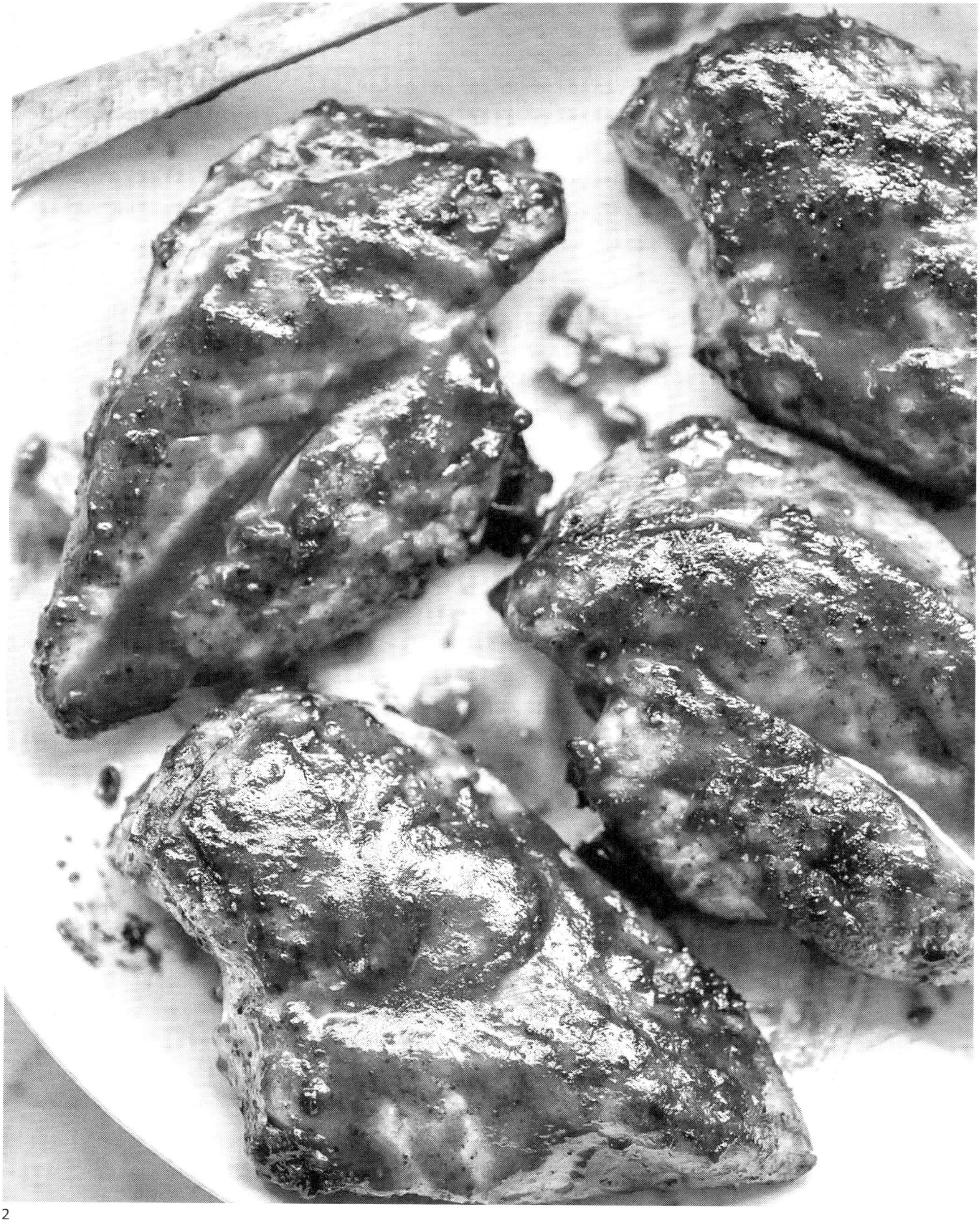

Table of Contents

Introduction 5

Ninja Foodi and Its Various Functions 6

Breakfast Recipes 8

Chocolate Oatmeal 8
Breakfast Casserole 9
Cinnamon Rolls 10
Fried Eggs 11
Ninja Foodi Yogurt 12
Breakfast Muffins 13
Hash Browns 14
Ninja Foodi Quiche 15

Snacks and Appetizers Recipes 16

French Fries 16
Ninja Foodi Kale Chips 17
Buffalo Cauliflower 18
Ninja Foodi Coconut Shrimp 19
Ninja Foodi Eggplant Chips 20
Buffalo Wings 21
Ninja Foodi Pizza Rolls 22
Ninja Foodi Roasted Potatoes 23
Easy Chickpeas 24
Ninja Foodi Corn Dog Bites 25
Ninja Foodi Tofu 26

Vegetables and Sides Recipes 27

Fried Rice 27
Veggie Pot Pie 28
Quinoa with Vegetables 29
Vegan Chili 31
Minestrone Soup 32
Baked Beans 33
Mashed Potatoes 35
Falafel 36
Spinach and Chickpea Stew 37
Stir-Fried Bok Choy 38

Fish and Seafood Recipes 39

Herbed Salmon 39
Shrimp Fajitas 40
Grilled Shrimp Foil Packs 41
Cajun Shrimp 42
Grilled Lobster Tail 43
Easy Catfish 44
Fish Tacos 45
Easy Salmon 46
Fish and Grits 47
Buffalo Tuna Cakes 48
Crispy Cod 49
Shrimp Risotto 50

Poultry Mains Recipes ... 51

Lemon Pesto Whole Chicken ... 51
Cream Cheese Shredded Chicken with Bacon ... 52
Apricot Chicken ... 53
Chicken Breast ... 54
Chicken with Roasted Potatoes ... 55
Teriyaki Chicken, Broccoli & Rice ... 56
Easy Turkey-Pesto Meatballs with Penne Pasta ... 57
Coq Au Vin ... 58
Chili-Ranch Chicken Wings ... 60
Chicken Cacciatore with Farfalle ... 61
Chicken Piccata Pasta ... 62
French Onion Chicken ... 63
Southwestern Roast Chicken ... 64
Lemon Pepper Chicken Legs ... 65

Beef, Pork, and Lamb Recipes ... 66

Perfect Roast Beef ... 66
Beef & Broccoli ... 67
Beef Stroganoff ... 68
Beef and Mushrooms Stew ... 69
Minced Beef and Rice Casserole ... 70
Corned Beef and Cabbage ... 71
Beef Stew & Dumplings ... 72
Pulled Pork ... 73
Sweet and Savory Pork fillet steak ... 74
Pepper Garlic Pork Fillet Steak ... 75
Crispy Pork Carnitas ... 76
Herbed Lamb Cutlet ... 77
Lamb with Mint ... 78
Roasted Lamb Cutlet ... 80

Dessert Recipes ... 81

Chocolate Chip Frying Pan Cookie ... 81
Apple Pie Filling ... 82
Zeppole ... 83
Brownies ... 84
Lemon Basil Scones ... 85
Courgette Bread ... 87
Rice Pudding ... 88
Pound Cake ... 89
Pumpkin Pie ... 90
Eggnog ... 91
Triple Chocolate Cheesecake ... 92

4 Weeks Meal Plan ... 94

1st week Meal Plan ... 94
2nd week Meal Plan ... 95
3rd week Meal Plan ... 96
4th week Meal Plan ... 97

Conclusion ... 98

Introduction

Ninja is one of the biggest competitors of instant pot for multi-purpose gadgets, has a new entry in the market. The Ninja Foodi Digital Air fryer also combines multiple other functions to act as a toaster oven, dehydrator, and a small countertop convection oven. Yes, you could even bake cookies in this air fryer!

Using the Ninja Foodi Air Fryer allows you to enjoy fried food that is actually healthy since it doesn't require oil. This great gadget serves as a countertop convection oven, dehydrator, and warmer.

The Foodi can pressure cook, slow cook, sauté, steam, and air fry. It also features Tender Crisp technology, which is a combination of pressure cooking and air frying that allows you to rapidly cook ingredients and finish off with a crispy texture. Good Housekeeping notes that this feature makes the Ninja Foodi stand out from the crowd. Though, since the Ninja Foodi hit the market, Instant Pot has created its own version: The Instant Pot Duo Crisp, which pressure cooks and air fries.

Ninja Foodi and Its Various Functions

Pressure cooker function: The pressure cooker is essentially a saucepan equipped with a sealed lid with a valve (the black valve that turns from the seal to the vent) for release the pressure, and a breather/button (the red button), Pressure is on This article refers to an electric pressure cooker such as the Ninja Foodi: The quick cook function is an excellent way to speed up the cooking process. The food is usually prepared in 1/3 of the time, it would take on the stove or in the oven. For example, an entire chicken takes about 20 minutes per pound to be fried. Under pressure, it should take about 5 minutes per pound. In this entire chicken recipe with the instant pot, I went with 4 minutes per pound plus two additional minutes. In the end, and honestly, I do not think I need the extra additional minutes.

Steam function: I like all the functions of Ninja Foodi and find each of them useful, but the steam feature is my option to warm leftovers that are not cooked outdoors. I just put what I want to warm with aluminum foil on the lid of the aluminum molds and place it with 2 cups of water on the bottom of the grid (high or low position). I set the steam function for 5 to 10 minutes, depending on the density of the food I eat, and that's it! A perfectly roasted food that stores moisture without overcooking. The steam function differs from the quick-cooking function because steam can escape during cooking. It is an excellent option for vegetables, delicate fish, and rice. You can also remove the lid during cooking to control the food. However, be careful, and open it, because a lot of steam has accumulated, and it is hot.

Slow Cooking function: As if there were not enough applications for the Ninja Foodi, it even has a Slow Cooking function. You can set the temperature to high or low, and remember to set the black valve to air when you are cooking slowly. We want to release the accumulated steam. Although most of us love the speed of quick-cooking, the slow cooking function is undoubtedly useful. The other day I tried to decide for dinner and found that all my meat was frozen. Of course, I was able to cook frozen meat, but it was early in the day and I decided to try a pork fillet in the slow cooker. I added the ingredients, put them on top of it and my pork and vegetable curry (I added them in the last hour) was ready on time for dinner. It was a dinner without hands and delicious.

Sear/Sauté function: I like this feature of Ninja Foodi and use it always. Now meat is no longer a warranty, as in a stainless-steel pot, but I think the warranty is enough for what I use. You can use this setting at many different temperatures, although I tend to use the higher setting. It is ideal for frying vegetables before adding broth and other ingredients to prepare soups or stews. Heat the milk to make home-made yogurt at Ninja Foodi.

Air Crisp Function: One of the main selling points of Ninja Foodi is the Air Crisp feature! It works very well, I have never had an air fryer in front of the Ninja Foodi, so I can not compare an independent fryer with the Foodi, but I love this feature. One of the benefits of Ninja Foodi is that you can cook under pressure and brown or burn the meat with the fresh air function.

Bake/Roast function: The cooking/frying function of the Ninja Foodi works like a small convection oven. I did several tests with this feature because people said they burned their food when they used the cooking/frying feature. What I found is that the temperatures are accurate. If the temperature is set to 350 ° F, it is heated to 350 ° F. Why cook faster? The fan circulates the hot air. When cooking in a hot air oven, the food is faster. Sometimes this is great and sometimes, as with bread and the densest foods, too much brown food may come out and remain uncooked in the middle. To remedy this, I suggest you lower the temperature by 10 ° C. Example: If your cornbread recipe requires a temperature of 425 ° F, set the cooking/frying function to 375 ° F and cook in the oven. Displayed temperature. Remember that you can lift the lid at any time to check the progress. Do not overdo it, as you release the heat each time you open the lid.

Broil Function: There is a difference between the cooking/frying function and the frying function. There! Heats more than 25 ° F as the cooking/frying function. Although you can not set a temperature for the roast function, it will reach about 425 ° F after 15 minutes. I will certainly use this feature more intensively soon. I have not had time to do the tests on this topic yet.

Breakfast Recipes

Chocolate Oatmeal

Prep Time: 05minutes.
Cook Time: 05 minutes.
Serves: 2

Ingredients:

- 200 g quick oats
- 400 g chocolate almond milk
- 50 g chocolate chips optional

Preparation:

1. Spray the inside of your baking dishes with non-stick spray.
2. Add the oatmeal and chocolate almond milk to your bowl and stir. Pour 1.5 c of water into your saucepan and lower the saucer with the full container on it.
3. Place the lid on the pressure cooker (the one that is not attached) and close the steam valve.
4. Put it on high pressure for 5 minutes.
5. Make a quick pitch, stir, serve with chocolate chips and strawberries on top!

Serving Suggestion: Serve the Chocolate Oatmeal with choice of fruit

Variation Tip: use normal milk if not getting almond milk

Nutritional Information Per Serving:
Calories 296| Fat 11g |Sodium 351mg | Carbs 43g | Fiber 5g | Sugar 14g | Protein 7g

Breakfast Casserole

Prep Time: 10 minutes.
Cook Time: 15 minutes.
Serves: 4

Ingredients:

- 1 lb minced Sausage
- 50 g Diced White Onion
- 1 Diced red Pepper
- 8 Whole Eggs, Beaten
- 60 g Shredded Colby Jack Cheese
- ½ tsp Fennel Seed
- ¼ tsp Garlic Salt

Preparation:

1. If you are using Ninja Foodi, use the stir-fry function to brown the sausage in the Ninja Foodi pot.
2. Add the onion and paprika and sauté with the chopped sausage until the vegetables are tender and the sausage is cooked through.
3. Use the 8.75-inch Frying pan or air frying pan to spray with non-stick cooking spray.
4. Place the minced sausage mixture in the bottom of the pan.
5. Cover evenly with cheese.
6. For eggs, whip evenly over cheese and sausage.
7. Distribute the fennel seeds and garlic salt evenly over the eggs.
8. Place the rack in the lower position on the Ninja Foodi, then place the tray on top.
9. Place on Air Crisp for 15 minutes at 390 degrees.
10. If using a deep fryer, place the pan directly in the frying basket and cook at 390 degrees for 15 minutes.
11. Take out carefully and serve.

Serving Suggestion: Serve the Breakfast Casserole with dipping sauce

Variation Tip: use any kind of minced meat if not available sausage

Nutritional Information Per Serving:
Calories 282| Fat 23g |Sodium 682mg | Carbs 3g | Fiber 0g | Sugar 2g | Protein 17g

Cinnamon Rolls

Prep Time: 20 minutes.
Cook Time: 10 minutes.
Serves: 8

Ingredients:

- 1 Can of Pillsbury Cinnamon Rolls (8-Count)
- Coconut Oil Cooking Spray

Preparation:

1. Spray the basket of the Ninja Foodi with the oil.
2. Place the cinnamon rolls equally into the basket.
3. Set aside the icing.
4. Air Fry or Air Crisp the cinnamon rolls for 8 minutes at 360 degrees.
5. Check these around 7 minutes to be sure they are cooking well due to the heat difference in air fryers.
6. Once done, remove and top with icing.
7. Serve.

Serving Suggestion: Serve the Cinnamon Rolls with coffee

Variation Tip: use any cooking spray in case not having coconut oil

Nutritional Information Per Serving:
Calories 52| Fat 3g |Sodium 85mg | Carbs 3g | Fiber 0g | Sugar 2g | Protein 0g

Fried Eggs

Prep Time: 01 minutes.
Cook Time: 05 minutes.
Serves: 4

Ingredients:

- 4 Eggs
- Aluminium Foil
- Olive Oil Cooking Spray

Preparation:

1. Make an aluminium bag that fits in the air fryer, one sheet per egg.
2. Brush with olive oil spray and whip an egg in the bag.
3. Put it in the Ninja Foodi.
4. Cook at 390 * F for 6 minutes or until cooked through, depending on your preference.
5. Take out carefully and serve with other dishes.

Serving Suggestion: Serve the Fried Eggs with salad or sausage

Variation Tip: use coconut oil in case not having olive oil

Nutritional Information Per Serving:
Calories 135| Fat 12g |Sodium 71mg | Carbs 0g | Fiber 0g | Sugar 0g | Protein 7g

Ninja Foodi Yogurt

Prep Time: 10 minutes.
Cook Time: 8 hr.
Serves: 12

Ingredients:

- 3.25 lb skimmed milk
- 2 tbsp. Greek yogurt plain with live active cultures
- 1 tbsp. vanilla
- fresh fruit optional, stir in when chilled and done

Preparation:

1. Mix 2 tablespoons of Greek yogurt with 1 cup of ultra-filtered whole milk until smooth.
2. Then add the Greek yogurt mixture to the remaining milk in your pressure cooker and stir. Add the vanilla.
3. Use your stir-fry function, set it to Normal and add your milk. Prepare a thermometer. Stir intermittently so as not to overheat at the lower test temperature, you want to heat the milk to 180 degrees F.
4. Then turn off the pot and refrigerate the milk until it is between 112- and 115-degrees F. Then add your yogurt. Add vanilla or any other extract for flavoured yogurt, omit it for plain yogurt.
5. Close the lid, keep the steam valve OPEN and let stand for 8 hours. Then remove the inner pot and let it cool to room temperature on the counter.
6. Then cover the top with Cling film and place in the refrigerator overnight or 8 hours.

Serving Suggestion: Serve the Yogurt with granola

Variation Tip: use almond or coconut milk if want low carb

Nutritional Information Per Serving:
Calories 80| Fat 4g |Sodium 54mg | Carbs 6g | Fiber 2.6g | Sugar 6g | Protein 4g

Breakfast Muffins

Prep Time: 15 minutes.
Cook Time: 10 minutes.
Serves: 4

Ingredients:

- 125 g Self-raising flour
- 25 g sugar
- 1/8 tsp cinnamon
- 20 ml milk
- 1½ tbsp. butter melted
- 1 egg
- 2 tsp vanilla
- 95 g blueberries fresh or frozen and defrosted

Preparation:

1. Combine the wet ingredients in a bowl, then stir in the flour and cinnamon. Once the mixture is mixed, gently fold in the berries. If using packaging, follow package directions for ingredients needed for mixing.
2. Preheat the Ninja Foodi to 340 degrees F for 5 minutes.
3. Place 3/4 of the silicone muffin cups in the basket.
4. Bake for 12-14 minutes or until toothpick comes out clean in center.

Serving Suggestion: Serve the Breakfast Muffins with omelette

Variation Tip: use all-purpose flour substitute of self-rising flour

Nutritional Information Per Serving:
Calories 143| Fat 5g |Sodium 51mg | Carbs 20g| Fiber 1g | Sugar 8g | Protein 3g

Hash Browns

Prep Time: 15 minutes.
Cook Time: 20 minutes.
Serves: 4

Ingredients:

- 2 potatoes peeled and shredded, russets
- 1 small onion diced
- ½ tsp salt
- ¼ tsp pepper
- 125 g cheese shredded, optional

Preparation:

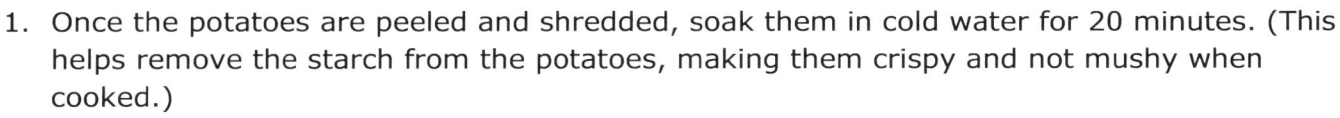

1. Once the potatoes are peeled and shredded, soak them in cold water for 20 minutes. (This helps remove the starch from the potatoes, making them crispy and not mushy when cooked.)
2. Drain the potatoes and remove as much water as possible. Place on a stack of paper towels and squeeze to remove moisture. Combine potatoes, onions, salt and pepper in a large bowl.
3. Mix well. Pour the mixture into the greased Ninja Foodi basket. Air fry for 20 minutes at 400 ° F, stirring every 5 minutes.
4. Top with grated cheese of your choice and air fry for 2-3 minutes until melted. Alternatively, you can put the cheese on a plate and melt it in the microwave.

Serving Suggestion: Serve the Hash Browns with dipping sauce

Variation Tip: use sweet potato instead of potato

Nutritional Information Per Serving:
Calories 85| Fat 4g |Sodium 505mg | Carbs 3g | Fiber 1g | Sugar 1g | Protein 5g

Ninja Foodi Quiche

Prep Time: 10 minutes.
Cook Time: 10 minutes.
Serves: 8

Ingredients:

- 3 eggs
- ¼ Red pepper diced
- 60 g onions diced
- 2 tbsp. milk
- 2-3 grape tomatoes halved
- 1 tbsp. sun dried tomatoes
- 2 tbsp. cheese shredded
- ¼ tsp thyme
- ¼ tsp salt
- 1/8 tsp pepper
- olive oil spray

Preparation:

1. Preheat the Ninja Foodi to 360 ° F for 5 minutes.
2. whip the eggs in a bowl, then add all the other ingredients and stir.
3. Spray a 4-inch pan with non-stick spray, then pour in the egg mixture.
4. Place the pan in the Ninja Foodi's basket for a total of 8 minutes and turn it over halfway through cooking.
5. Remove, let cool in the mold for at least 3 minutes before unmoulding.

Serving Suggestion: Serve the Quiche with dipping sauce

Variation Tip: add your choice of vegetables

Nutritional Information Per Serving:
Calories 95| Fat 6g |Sodium 245mg | Carbs 3g | Fiber 1g | Sugar 2g | Protein 7g

Snacks and Appetizers Recipes

French Fries

Prep Time: 15 minutes.
Cook Time: 25 minutes.
Serves: 8

Ingredients:

- 5 medium potatoes russet, 1.5 lbs.
- 3 tbsp olive oil
- ½ tsp seasoned salt

Preparation:

1. Wash, cut the potatoes into strips one by one (like French fries), leave the skin on place on paper towels and wrap to remove as much moisture as possible from the outside
2. Put in a bowl and rub with olive oil.
3. Put them in the air fryer basket of your Ninja Foodi
4. Close the cover (the one attached), turn on the machine.
5. Press the air crisp button. Regulate the temperature. to 390 with a duration of 20-23 minutes. Turn 3 times during the cooking time (about 7 minutes).
6. Add a few more minutes if you want them to be more golden / crispier or take them out earlier if you want them to be very lightly browned. For best results, remove immediately when finished.
7. Take out and serve.

Serving Suggestion: Serve French Fries with ketchup

Variation Tip: use sweet potatoes if want low carb

Nutritional Information Per Serving:
Calories 165| Fat 6g |Sodium 211mg | Carbs 22g | Fiber 4g | Sugar 0g | Protein 4g

Ninja Foodi Kale Chips

Prep Time: 10 minutes.
Cook Time: 05 minutes.
Serves: 6

Ingredients:

- 1 bunch kale curly kale is best, washed, dried, remove stems
- 2 tbsp. olive oil
- ¼ tsp seasoned salt or ½ tsp. dry ranch dressing mix

Preparation:

1. Wash your kale and place it on the counter on paper towels to dry completely.
2. Remove the middle stems and cut the leaves into bite-sized chunks, they will shrink.
3. Put the pieces in a bowl and drizzle with olive oil, sprinkle with seasoned salt or ranch dressing.
4. Massage the leaves with your hands with salt and oil.
5. Place half of your prepared package in your Air fryer basket
6. Close the fryer lid (attached to Ninja Foodi) and press air crisp 390-degree for 2 minutes.
7. Lift the lid and flip the kale chips to make them evenly crisp.
8. Set the cool air to 390 degrees for an additional 2 minutes (or set it to 4 minutes and turn it halfway). Then take it out and do the same with the second half of your batch of prepared kale.
9. The kale chips should be crispy on both sides. If you have a slightly larger bunch, you may need to add a minute at the end to make sure all the pieces are very crisp like chips. Take advantage of it right away for better results.

Serving Suggestion: Serve the Kale Chips with tea

Variation Tip: use coconut oil if not getting olive oil

Nutritional Information Per Serving:
Calories 51| Fat 4g |Sodium 105mg | Carbs 1g | Fiber 1g | Sugar 2g | Protein 7g

Buffalo Cauliflower

Prep Time: 10 minutes.
Cook Time: 10 minutes.
Serves: 8

Ingredients:

- 2.2 lbs Cauliflower Florets
- 57 g Butter, Melted
- 125 g Buffalo Sauce
- 250g Gluten-Free Bread Crumbs
- 1 Tbsp. Garlic Powder
- 1 Tsp Salt
- ½ Tsp Pepper
- Olive Oil Spray

Preparation:

1. Combine butter and Buffalo sauce in a large bowl.
2. Add the cauliflower and cover well.
3. Combine breadcrumbs, garlic powder, salt and pepper in another bowl.
4. Place each cauliflower wrap in the breadcrumb mixture to coat.
5. Spray the Ninja Foodi frying basket with olive oil spray.
6. Place the cauliflower evenly in the air fryer basket, this should be done in 2 portions, it should fit in the middle of the cauliflower
7. cook for 12-15 minutes at 350 * F, until the cauliflower is golden brown, cooked through and crispy. If you like, you can put another coat of olive oil spray on top to give it a crispier look and texture
8. When you're done, carefully remove the extra batch and cook it.
9. Serve with your choice of sides such as celery and ranch dressing.

Serving Suggestion: Serve the Buffalo Cauliflower with dipping sauce

Variation Tip: use Regular Bread Crumbs

Nutritional Information Per Serving:
Calories 195| Fat 11g |Sodium 1245mg | Carbs 13g | Fiber 3g | Sugar 3g | Protein 4g

Ninja Foodi Coconut Shrimp

Prep Time: 05 minutes.
Cook Time: 10 minutes.
Serves: 12

Ingredients:

- 1lb Cooked, Peeled, and Deveined Tail-On Shrimp
- 125g Gluten-Free Almond Flour
- 2 Eggs, Beaten
- 125g Gluten-Free or Regular Panko Breadcrumbs
- 3/4 Cup Sweetened Shredded Coconut
- Olive Oil Spray

Preparation:

1. Start by preparing the ingredients, a bowl for the flour, another for the egg.
2. Take an extra bowl for the breadcrumbs and coconut, add a pinch of salt if you prefer that bowl too.
3. Dip each shrimp in the flour, then in the egg and drain the excess.
4. Then garnish with breadcrumbs.
5. Spray the Ninja Foodi air fryer basket with cooking spray and place the shrimp in the fryer, brush the shrimp with cooking spray.
6. Heat the Ninja Foodi air fryer to 355 * F and cook the shrimp for 10 minutes.
7. Check halfway through cooking and sprinkle with additional olive oil if desired.

Serving Suggestion: Serve the Coconut Shrimp with ketchup

Variation Tip: use Regular plain flour if not want to use almond flour

Nutritional Information Per Serving:
Calories 153| Fat 4g |Sodium 361mg | Carbs 18g | Fiber 1g | Sugar 3g | Protein 10g

Ninja Foodi Eggplant Chips

Prep Time: 10 minutes.
Cook Time: 10 minutes.
Serves: 12

Ingredients:

- 1 Aubergine
- 2 Eggs, Beaten
- 35g Plain Flour
- 30g Breadcrumbs
- 30g Grated Parmesan Cheese
- 1 Tbsp. Italian Seasoning
- Olive Oil Cooking Spray

Preparation:

1. Cut the Aubergine into thin slices of about 1/8 "and set aside.
2. Put the flour in a small bowl.
3. In a small bowl, break and whip the eggs or whip well to combine.
4. Finally, combine the breadcrumbs, cheese and spices in a third bowl.
5. Dip each Aubergine slice in the flour mixture, shaking off the excess.
6. Dip it in the eggs, shake off the excess and cover with breadcrumbs.
7. Place a piece of foil in the Ninja Foodi Air fryer basket with a layer of olive oil spray. Make sure it is rolled up on its side to allow air to circulate.
8. Place the Aubergine in the deep fryer. I was able to do 4 at a time using this method, it varies by size.
9. Add another coat of spray on the Aubergine.
10. Bake 5 minutes at 390 degrees.
11. Gently flip the Aubergine and brush it with an olive oil spray. Then cook for another 5 minutes.

Serving Suggestion: Serve the Aubergine Chips with ketchup

Variation Tip: add almond flour if want gluten free

Nutritional Information Per Serving:
Calories 115| Fat 3g |Sodium 85mg | Carbs 13g | Fiber 2g | Sugar 2g | Protein 4g

Buffalo Wings

P rep Time: 05 minutes.
Cook Time: 20 minutes.
Serves: 12

Ingredients:

- 6-12 Chicken Wings,
- Olive Oil Cooking Spray
- 4 Tbsp. Melted Butter
- 125 g Buffalo Sauce
- Salt/Pepper to Taste

Preparation:

1. Coat the Ninja Foodi basket with cooking spray.
2. Place the chicken wings in the basket and cook at 198 °C for 20 minutes, flip after 10 minutes.
3. The internal temperature should be at least 74°C
4. While cooking, melt the butter and mix with the Buffalo sauce.
5. Once the wings are cooked, soak and cover with the Buffalo sauce mixture and let sit in a saucepan for about 2 to 5 minutes.
6. Add salt and pepper to taste.

Serving Suggestion: Serve the Buffalo Wings with mayonnaise

Variation Tip: use turkey wings

Nutritional Information Per Serving:
Calories 440| Fat 16g |Sodium 1345mg | Carbs 10g | Fiber 1g | Sugar 1g | Protein 17g

Ninja Foodi Pizza Rolls

Prep Time: 1 minutes.
Cook Time: 10 minutes.
Serves: 4

Ingredients:

- 1 Package Frozen Pizza Rolls
- Olive Oil Cooking Spray

Preparation:

1. Spray the Ninja Foodi basket with olive oil cooking spray.
2. Place an even layer of frozen pizza rolls in the basket.
3. Put another layer of olive oil in cooking spray on the pizza rolls.
4. Air fry 8 minutes at 198 °C, I suggest you check them after 6 minutes as all fryers heat up differently.
5. Then carefully remove and serve.

Serving Suggestion: Serve the Pizza Rolls with dipping sauce

Variation Tip: add coconut oil

Nutritional Information Per Serving:
Calories 41| Fat 4g |Sodium 20mg | Carbs 2g | Fiber 0g | Sugar 0g | Protein 0g

Ninja Foodi Roasted Potatoes

Prep Time: 10 minutes.
Cook Time: 30 minutes.
Serves: 8

Ingredients:

- 4 Large Potatoes
- ½ Tbsp. Olive Oil
- 1 Tbsp. Rosemary

Preparation:

1. Cut the potatoes in half lengthwise and cut them into smaller pieces.
2. Put the potatoes in the zip lock bag with the olive oil and rosemary.
3. Close it and shake it.
4. Cover the bottom of your Ninja Foodi with foil and spray it with non-stick cooking spray if desired.
5. Evenly pour the potatoes into your Ninja Foodi and cook at 198 °C for 20 minutes.

Serving Suggestion: Serve the Quiche with dipping sauce

Variation Tip: add your choice of vegetables

Nutritional Information Per Serving:
Calories 95| Fat 6g |Sodium 245mg | Carbs 3g | Fiber 1g | Sugar 2g | Protein 7g

Easy Chickpeas

Prep Time: 05 minutes.
Cook Time: 10 minutes.
Serves: 4

Ingredients:

- 1lb tinned Chickpeas (Rinsed and Drained)
- Cooking Oil Spray of Choice (Grapeseed, Coconut, Avocado, Etc.)
- 2 Tsp Seasoning of Choice

Preparation:

1. Rinse and drain the chickpeas and place them in a bowl.
2. Brush with cooking spray of your choice and season.
3. Place evenly in the Ninja Foodi.
4. Bake at 198 °C for 10-12 minutes, then check and monitor after 6 minutes as all fryers heat differently.

Serving Suggestion: Serve the Easy Chickpeas with tea or coffee

Variation Tip: use seasoning of your choice

Nutritional Information Per Serving:
Calories 195| Fat 7g |Sodium 1039mg | Carbs 26g | Fiber 7g | Sugar 2g | Protein 8g

Ninja Foodi Corn Dog Bites

Prep Time: 10 minutes.
Cook Time: 10 minutes.
Serves: 14

Ingredients:

- 4 hot dogs cut
- 280g flour
- 96g corn Flour
- 50 g sugar
- 2 tsp Bicarbonate of soda
- ½ tsp salt
- 250 ml milk
- 1 egg
- 60 ml oil optional, have with or without it when I was out and turned out similarly

Preparation:

1. Combine the dry ingredients for the cornbread, then add the milk, oil and egg and mix well.
2. Spray the inside of your egg mold with non-stick spray (good). Fill each pocket halfway with the cornbread mixture.
3. Cut each hot dog into 4 equal pieces and press 1 piece into the center of each hole filled with cornbread.
4. Cover the egg pan with foil
5. Pour 354 ml of water into your Ninja Foodi. Place the egg on a trivet with handles and lower into your pot.
6. Close the lid and the steam valve and put on high pressure for 9 minutes. Then let it steam naturally for 5 minutes. Then let the rest of the steam escape.
7. Immediately remove the foil and let cool in the pan for 3 to 4 minutes to keep them intact when you remove them.
8. Then turn and gently squeeze the lower pockets so that every bite of corn comes out.

Serving Suggestion: Serve the Corn Dog with sauce

Variation Tip: add your choice of milk

Nutritional Information Per Serving:
Calories 170| Fat 7g |Sodium 184mg | Carbs 21g | Fiber 1g | Sugar 4g | Protein 4g

Ninja Foodi Tofu

Prep Time: 15 minutes.

Cook Time: 15 minutes.

Serves: 8

Ingredients:

- 396 g tofu extra firm is best
- 60 ml soy sauce used low sodium
- 1 tbsp. garlic chili sauce
- 1 tbsp. sesame oil
- 1 tbsp. minced garlic
- sesame seeds garnish
- spring onions diced, garnish

Preparation:

1. Wrap the tofu block in light muslin or folded paper towels, squeeze it firmly but do not break it. You want to remove as much moisture as possible with this step.
2. Cut the tofu into 1 "cubes and place them in a shallow bowl.
3. Combine marinade ingredients in a bowl and pour over the tofu bites. Let stand 5 to 10 minutes to absorb the sauce.
4. Preheat the fryer to 380 degrees F for 5 minutes.
5. Spray the inside of the basket and place the pieces inside so they don't overlap.
6. Set the time to 12 minutes, flip each piece to 6 minute.
7. When they're as crispy as you want, take them out and garnish with sesame seeds and spring onion.

Serving Suggestion: Serve the tofu with dipping sauce

Variation Tip: use chicken

Nutritional Information Per Serving:
Calories 38| Fat 2.5g |Sodium 115mg | Carbs 1.7g | Fiber 0.7g | Sugar 0.2g | Protein 2.9g

Vegetables and Sides Recipes

Fried Rice

Prep Time: 15 minutes.
Cook Time: 15 minutes.
Serves: 4

Ingredients:

- 1 tbsp. oil
- garlic crushed
- 370 g rice, rinsed well
- 500 ml water
- 1 tbsp. soy sauce
- ½ cup frozen vegetables of choice

Preparation:

1. Add the rice, 500 ml of water and the rest of the ingredients to the pot of the Ninja Foodi.
2. Close the pressure button and make sure the valve is sealed
3. Set to high pressure for 3 minutes and press start
4. When pressure cooking is complete, naturally release the pressure for 11 minutes, then quickly release the remaining pressure.
5. Mix everything well, serve and enjoy!

Serving Suggestion: Serve the Fried Rice with salad

Variation Tip: use brown rice or quinoa

Nutritional Information Per Serving:
Calories 381| Fat 4g |Sodium 235mg | Carbs 74.5g | Fiber 1.7g | Sugar 0.2g | Protein 6.9g

Veggie Pot Pie

Prep Time: 10 minutes.
Cook Time: 25 minutes.
Serves: 8

Ingredients:

- 4 tablespoons unsalted butter
- ½ large onion, diced
- 1 ½ cups diced carrots (about 2 large carrots)
- 1 ½ cups diced celery (about 3 stalks celery)
- 2 cloves garlic, minced
- 3 medium potatoes diced
- 250 ml vegetable broth
- 70 g frozen peas
- 70 g frozen corn
- 1 tablespoon chopped fresh Italian parsley
- 2 teaspoons fresh thyme leaves
- 34 g flour
- 64 g Double cream
- salt
- pepper
- 1 prepared pie crust

Preparation:

1. Press the SEAR / SAUTE button and set MD: HI. Press START and let the ninja Foodi preheat for 5 minutes.
2. Melt butter in a Ninja Foodi pan. Add onions, carrots and celery to melted butter; sauté until tender (about 3 minutes).
3. Add the garlic to the vegetables and cook, stirring constantly, until they smell the scent (about 30 seconds). Press STOP.
4. Put the potatoes and the broth in the pot. Stir, then place the pressure cooker lid on the pot. Place the valve in the SEAL position.
5. Select PRESSURE and set it to HIGH for 5 minutes. Press Start.
6. When you're done, do a quick release. Remove the cap.
7. Add the peas, corn, thyme and parsley to the pot. Sprinkle with flour and mix well. Add the Double cream.
8. Select SEAR / SAUTE and set it to MD: HI. Press Start. Cook, stirring constantly, until the sauce is thick and hot (about 2 to 3 minutes).
9. Press the STOP button. Season the mixture with S&P to taste.
10. Pour the pie crust over the vegetable mixture. Fold the edges of the base to fit inside the pot. Make a small ventilation hole in the middle of the crust.
11. Close the lid to grill, then select BROIL. Set the time to 10 minutes and press START.
12. When the time has elapsed, place the inner pot on a heat-resistant surface. Let the cake stand for 10 minutes, then serve. Enjoy!

Serving Suggestion: Serve the Veggie Pot Pie with dipping salad

Variation Tip: use any kind of vegetables of your choice

Nutritional Information Per Serving:
Calories 238| Fat 12.5g |Sodium 303mg | Carbs 27g | Fiber 3g | Sugar 2g | Protein 4.9g

Quinoa with Vegetables

Prep Time: 10 minutes.
Cook Time: 05 minutes.
Serves: 8

Ingredients:

Spice Blend

- 1 tsp sea salt
- 1 tsp basil leaves
- ½ oregano
- ½ parsley
- ½ black pepper

Quinoa with Vegetables

- 1 Tbsp. olive oil
- 1 bulb garlic
- 1½ cups quinoa
- 1 Tbsp. Minors Vegetable Base
- 1 cup water room temp
- ½ cup artichokes tinned in water, drained
- 5 mini red peppers or 2 bell peppers (red/yellow/orange)
- 2.5-ounce black olives sliced in juice
- 1 cup spring onions chopped
- 2½ cups Normandy Blend Vegetable Mix frozen
- 2 Tbsp. green olive juice
- ½ cup green olives
- 2 small tomatoes

Preparation:

1. Remove the garlic cloves and onion and peel them. Cut the pepper into slices. Chop the spring onions.
2. Put the Ninja Foodi on high sear / sauté. Add 1 tablespoon of olive oil, the garlic and the rinsed quinoa. Let the pot heat up and stir the mixture about every minute. You can roast the quinoa and garlic for 2 to 7 minutes.
3. Once the preparation is complete and the quinoa toasted for 2 to 7 minutes, add the vegetable base and stir. Add 1 cup of water and stir.
4. Add the spice blend, artichokes, peppers, black olives (with juice), spring onions, frozen vegetables and mix.
5. Cut the green olives in half and add them to the pan with the 2 tablespoons of green olive juice. Slice the tomatoes and add them to the pot. Stir.
6. Replace the pressure cap and turn the valve to seal. Increase the pressure for 1 minute. When the time is up, allow the pot to loosen naturally for 10 minutes. Release the

remaining pressure. If you want your quinoa to cook a little longer, just replace the pressure cap with the vent valve and leave it on the reheat level for a few minutes and the quinoa will continue to cook.
7. Serve, garnish with chopped spring onions and feta cheese. Serve and enjoy!

Serving Suggestion: Serve the Quinoa with Vegetables with salad

Variation Tip: use rice

Nutritional Information Per Serving:
Calories 238| Fat 9g |Sodium 1115mg | Carbs 35g | Fiber 7g | Sugar 2g | Protein 7g

Vegan Chili

Prep Time: 10 minutes.
Cook Time: 50 minutes.
Serves: 8

Ingredients:

- 1 tablespoon olive oil
- 1 medium onion, diced
- 3 cloves garlic, minced
- 1 (28-ounce) tinned crushed tomatoes
- 1 cup vegetable broth
- 4 large carrots, chopped (about 180 g)
- 5 stalks celery, chopped (about 180 g)
- 3 medium russet potatoes, chopped (about 380g)
- 256 grams cooked kidney beans
- 256 grams cooked black beans
- 164 g corn kernels
- 1 tablespoon tamari
- 1-3 tbsp. chili powder, added to taste
- salt and black pepper to taste

Preparation:

1. Select SEAR / SAUTE in Ninja Foodi and set MD: HI. Preheat for 5 minutes.
2. Add olive oil, onion and garlic to the pot and sauté for 5 minutes, stirring occasionally, until lightly browned.
3. Add the rest of the ingredients (except the cornbread dough) to the pot.
4. Install the pressure plug and make sure the drain valve is in the SEAL position. Select PRESSURE and set HIGH. Set the time to 15 minutes and select START / STOP to start.
5. When pressure cooking is complete, quickly release the valve by moving the pressure relief valve to the VENT position. Carefully remove the cap when the device is depressurized.
6. Stir the chili quickly. Use a spoon to pour about half of the Mini Muffin Vegan Cornbread Dough over the chili pepper (see note in Vegan Cornbread Recipe for what to do with leftover dough).
7. Close the lid to grill. Select BAKE / ROAST, set the temperature to 375 ° F and the time to 12 minutes. Select START / STOP to begin.

Serving Suggestion: Serve the chilli with rice

Variation Tip: use chicken

Nutritional Information Per Serving:
Calories 438| Fat 3.5g |Sodium 535mg | Carbs 87.3g | Fiber 31.4g | Sugar 11.2g | Protein 27.9g

Minestrone Soup

Prep Time: 25 minutes.
Cook Time: 60 minutes.
Serves: 8

Ingredients:

- 3 ½ tbsp. Olive Oil extra virgin, divided
- 1 Large Yellow Onion chopped
- 2 Ribs of Celery chopped
- 2 Carrots peeled and chopped
- 1 Courgette chopped
- 2 tbsp. Minced Garlic
- 1 tbsp. Italian Seasoning
- ½ tsp Red Pepper Flakes
- 28 oz. Roasted Diced Tomatoes
- 15 oz Tomato Sauce can
- 6 cups Vegetable Broth
- 2 (15 oz) Dark Red Kidney Beans cans, drained and rinsed
- 15 oz Cannellini Beans can, drained and rinsed
- ½ cup Cut Runner beans frozen
- 2 Bay Leaves
- 112g Cellentani Pasta dry,
- 120g Baby Spinach
- Juice of One Lemon
- Salt and Pepper to taste
- Fresh Parsley as Garnish chopped, to taste, optional

Preparation:

1. Heat a large saucepan over medium heat, add 3 tbsp. Olive oil. Add the onion, celery, carrot and Courgette. Season lightly with salt and pepper. Fry for about 7 minutes.
2. Add the chopped garlic. Fry another 2 minutes. Add Italian seasoning and red pepper flakes, sauté for one minute.
3. Add the diced tomatoes, tomato sauce, vegetable broth, kidney beans, cannellini beans, Runner beans and bay leaves. Mix and season with salt and pepper. Bring to a boil, then reduce to medium-low heat. Cook for 1 hour over low heat, stirring occasionally.
4. While the soup is simmering, cook the pasta in a separate pot until al dente. Flow out. Transfer to a bowl and add ½ tsp. Olive oil to prevent the dough from sticking. Put aside.
5. Remove the bay leaves. Add the spinach to the soup. Cook for five minutes. Then add the lemon juice and the cooked pasta. Cook for two more minutes.

Serving Suggestion: Serve the Minestrone Soup with sandwich

Variation Tip: use tubular pasta like elbow macaroni

Nutritional Information Per Serving:
Calories 198| Fat 1g |Sodium 1115mg | Carbs 30g | Fiber 0.7g | Sugar 8g | Protein 7g

Baked Beans

Prep Time: 10 minutes.
Cook Time: 60 minutes.
Serves: 4

Ingredients:

- 4 (16 ounce) Cannellini Beans or 4 cups dried beans already cooked
- 1 tablespoon olive oil
- 1 clove garlic, minced
- ½ medium onion, chopped
- 1 tablespoon Vegan Worcestershire sauce
- 112.33 g molasses
- 55 g Light brown sugar
- 2 tablespoons Light brown sugar, additional
- 60 g ketchup
- 2 teaspoon prepared yellow mustard
- 1 tablespoon barbecue sauce

Preparation:

1. Drain the tinned beans, rinse and place in a bowl. Put aside.
2. Take a small bowl and add your vegan Worcestershire sauce, molasses, Light brown sugar ketchup, yellow mustard and barbecue sauce to a bowl and mix until completely combined. Adjust the spices to your liking.
3. Turn on your Ninja Foodi machine. Make sure your pot is inside or your machine will not work.
4. Tap the jump method. Your temperature will automatically be raised. Set your temperature to medium high by pressing the down arrow. Then press start and let the oil heat up.
5. Add your chopped onions and garlic to your Ninja Foodi. Brown in a saucepan for about 3 to 5 minutes.
6. After cooking, press the down arrow at your stop on your Ninja Foodi until it indicates medium low. After 3 seconds you will hear a beep and the digital display will stop flashing. This is how you know your temperature is set. Leave the onions and garlic in your saucepan.
7. Add your beans to your pot with your molasses sauce mixture, scraping as much as possible into a bowl.
8. Take a cup of water and pour it into your bowl where the molasses sauce mixture was and mix. This is to help make sure the baked beans taste the best possible.
9. Pour the water mixture into your saucepan and stir until the beans have completely combined with the sauce. Taste and customize the taste as you like.
10. Cover the beans with the lid of the pressure cooker and close it completely. Make sure the valve is open, DO NOT seal it.

11. Simmer the beans for about 1 hour and 10 minutes, until the beans have thickened. Check half of the agitation.
12. When you're done, remove the cap and press the stopper on your Ninja Foodi. Then press the power button to turn off your device.
13. Let cool before serving.

Serving Suggestion: Serve the Baked Beans with potato salad

Variation Tip: use any type of beans

Nutritional Information Per Serving:
Calories 238| Fat 3g |Sodium 267mg | Carbs 47g | Fiber 0.7g | Sugar 45g | Protein 2.9g

Mashed Potatoes

Prep Time: 15 minutes.
Cook Time: 15 minutes.
Serves: 8

Ingredients:

- 3 Pounds Yukon Gold or Russet Potatoes, Peeled and Quartered
- 250 ml Water
- 120 g Cream
- 62g Sour Cream
- 4 Tbsp. Unsalted Butter
- 1 Tsp Garlic Salt or to Taste

Preparation:

1. Take the peeled and quartered potatoes and place them in the Ninja Foodi.
2. Add 1 cup of water.
3. Put the pressure cooker lid on the Ninja Foodi and secure it making sure the spout is "sealed".
4. Cook under high pressure for 10 minutes using the pressure cooker function.
5. Steam naturally 5 minutes after cooking time (do nothing).
6. After 5 minutes, quickly release the steam, then remove the lid.
7. Using a silicone potato masher, carefully mash the potatoes in the pan.
8. Add the rest of the ingredients and toss to combine the potatoes.
9. Close the lid attached to the Ninja Foodi and cook at 350 degrees for 3 minutes.
10. Open the lid and serve.

Serving Suggestion: Serve the Mashed Potatoes with chips

Variation Tip: use sweet potatoes

Nutritional Information Per Serving:
Calories 238| Fat 12g |Sodium 154mg | Carbs 27g | Fiber 3g | Sugar 2g | Protein 4g

Falafel

Prep Time: 15 minutes.
Cook Time: 45 minutes.
Serves: 4

Ingredients:

- 2 tin (425 g each) chickpeas, drained, rinsed
- 1 small onion, peeled, chopped
- 25 g bread crumbs
- ¼ cup flat-leaf Italian parsley, chopped
- 2 tablespoons lemon juice
- 2 cloves garlic, peeled smashed
- 2 teaspoons ground cumin
- 1 teaspoon Sea salt
- 1 teaspoon ground coriander
- ½ teaspoon ground black pepper
- 50 ml extra virgin olive oil, divided
- 1 large egg

Preparation:

1. Spread the chickpeas out on a paper towel lined sheet and let them air dry while you prepare the other ingredients.
2. Combine onion, breadcrumbs, parsley, lemon juice, garlic, cumin, salt, coriander and black pepper in a food processor and mix until onions are finely chopped.
3. Add the chickpeas, 3 tablespoons of oil and the egg and mix until the chickpeas are broken up and the mixture is combined.
4. Transfer the mixture to a large bowl and stir to make sure it is evenly mixed. Use a ¼ cup measuring cup to form 16 patties from the mixture. Cover and refrigerate for at least 30 minutes.
5. Brush the patties with the remaining oil on both sides.
6. Place the Cook & Crisp basket in the pot and close the lid to grill. Preheat the unit by selecting AIR CRISP, setting the temperature to 375 ° F and setting the time to 5 minutes. Select START / STOP to begin.
7. After 5 minutes, place half of the patties in the basket, leaving enough space. Close the cover. Select AIR CRISP, set the temperature to 375 ° F and the time to 22 minutes. Select START / STOP to begin.
8. After 11 minutes, put on flip flops to flip the patties. Close the lid to continue cooking.
9. When cooking is complete, remove the meatballs and repeat steps 7 and 8 with the remaining meatballs. Serve hot.

Serving Suggestion: Serve the Falafel with dipping sauce

Variation Tip: use gluten free bread crumbs

Nutritional Information Per Serving:
Calories 538| Fat 25.5g |Sodium 675mg | Carbs 68.7g | Fiber 18.7g | Sugar 12.2g | Protein 22.9g

Spinach and Chickpea Stew

Prep Time: 10 minutes.
Cook Time: 25 minutes.
Serves: 8

Ingredients:

- 1 tablespoon extra-virgin olive oil
- 1 yellow onion, diced 4 garlic cloves, minced
- 4 sweet potatoes, peeled and diced
- 4 cups vegetable broth
- 1 tin (400 g) fire-roasted diced tomatoes, drained
- 2 tins (425 g) each chickpea, drained
- 1½ teaspoons ground coriander
- Half teaspoon paprika
- ½ teaspoon salt
- ½ teaspoon fresh ground black pepper
- 4 cups baby spinach

Preparation:

1. Add the oil, onion and garlic to the pot, stir and cook for 5 minutes.
2. Then add the sweet potatoes, vegetable broth, tomatoes, chickpeas, cumin, coriander, paprika, salt and pepper to the Ninja Foodi pot. Replace the cap and close the pressure valves. Cook on HIGH for 8 minutes.
3. Quickly release the pressure and add the spinach to the pot.
4. Stir until tender.
5. Enjoy!

Serving Suggestion: Serve the Chickpea Stew with rice

Variation Tip: use kale as a substitute for spinach

Nutritional Information Per Serving:
Calories 166| Fat 2.9g |Sodium 605mg | Carbs 29.7g | Fiber 7g | Sugar 3.2g | Protein 5.9g

Stir-Fried Bok Choy

Prep Time: 05 minutes.
Cook Time: 10 minutes.
Serves: 4

Ingredients:

- 1 pound bok choy
- 1 tablespoon oyster sauce
- 3 tablespoons chicken broth or water
- 2 tablespoons peanut oil
- 2 teaspoon minced garlic
- 1 teaspoon salt

Preparation:

1. Separate the stems from the leaves, I just used a knife to cut the stalk.
2. Put the bok choy in a small bowl and wash it well.
3. After washing the bok choy add the oyster sauce, chicken broth, peanut oil, chopped garlic and salt. Make sure the leaves are well covered.
4. Connect the fryer and set the grill function. You need to heat the grill, but once it is hot enough, the machine prompts you to add food.
5. Add the bok choy.
6. Set the timer for 10 minutes.
7. Mix the bok choy every few minutes. Then it will not char.
8. Serve, serve and enjoy!

Serving Suggestion: Serve the Stir-Fried Bok Choy with quinoa

Variation Tip: use soy sauce if not getting oyster sauce

Nutritional Information Per Serving:
Calories 78| Fat 7.5g |Sodium 110mg | Carbs 3g | Fiber 1.7g | Sugar 1.2g | Protein 2g

Fish and Seafood Recipes

Herbed Salmon

Prep Time: 05 minutes.
Cook Time: 05 minutes.
Serves: 2

Ingredients:

- 2 (113 g each) Salmon Fillets
- 1 tsp. Herbes de Provence
- ¼ tsp Sea Salt
- ¼ tsp Black Pepper
- ¼ tsp Smoked Paprika
- 2 tbsp. Olive Oil
- 1 tbsp. Seasoned Butter,

Preparation:

1. Pat your steaks dry with a paper towel and smooth them out so that no bones are left.
2. Drizzle the fish with olive oil and rub on both sides of the arrangement
3. Mix the spices and sprinkle on both sides of the fish.
4. Turn on your Ninja Foodi to 390 degrees and cook for 5 to 8 minutes. I recommend starting with 5 minutes, checking the fish and adding 1 more minute until it flakes easily with a fork.
5. Melt the seasoned butter in the microwave for 30 seconds and pour over the fish before eating.

Serving Suggestion: Serve the Herbed Salmon with rice

Variation Tip: use any kind of fish

Nutritional Information Per Serving:
Calories 578| Fat 45.5g |Sodium 386mg | Carbs 2.2g | Fiber 10.7g | Sugar 1.5g | Protein 42g

Shrimp Fajitas

Prep Time: 10 minutes.
Cook Time: 22 minutes.
Serves: 12

Ingredients:

- 1 Pound Medium Shrimp, Tail-Off (Cooked, Frozen Shrimp)
- 2 Red Bell Pepper, Diced
- ½ Cup Sweet Onion, Diced
- 2 Tbsp. of Gluten-Free Fajita or Taco Seasoning
- Olive Oil Spray
- Corn Tortillas or Flour Tortillas

Preparation:

1. Spray the Ninja Foodi basket with olive oil spray or cover with foil.
2. If the shrimp are frozen with ice, run them under cold water to remove the ice.
3. Place the shrimp, peppers, onions and spices in the basket.
4. Add a layer of olive oil spray.
5. Mix everything.
6. Cook with the air fryer or the Air Crisp function of the Ninja Foodi for 12 minutes at 390 degrees.
7. Open the lid and spray and mix again.
8. Cook 10 minutes more.
9. Serve on hot tortillas.
10. This recipe uses cooked and frozen shrimp, it can also be made with raw shrimp, but it may take a few extra minutes of cooking.

Serving Suggestion: Serve the Shrimp Fajitas with quinoa

Variation Tip: use gluten free Tortillas

Nutritional Information Per Serving:
Calories 86| Fat 2g |Sodium 420mg | Carbs 6g | Fiber 1g | Sugar 1g | Protein 10g

Grilled Shrimp Foil Packs

Prep Time: 10 minutes.

Cook Time: 15 minutes.

Serves: 4

Ingredients:

- 340 g Small or Medium Shrimp (Peeled, Cooked, Tail-Off)
- 340 g Frozen Mixed Vegetables
- Seasoning of Choice
- Cooking Oil Spray (Grapeseed, Avocado, Coconut, Etc.)

Preparation:

1. Spray 4 sheets of aluminium foil with coconut oil spray.
2. Arrange shrimp and vegetables evenly on each sheet of foil to make 4 foil packages.
3. Season with a seasoning of your choice, such as a seasoning without added salt or lemon pepper. Add a layer of cooking spray.
4. Preheat the Ninja Foodi Grill with the grill function to HIGH.
5. Place the foil wraps on the grill and cook on the GRILL for 15 minutes on the highest setting.

Serving Suggestion: Serve the Grilled Shrimp Foil Packs with rice or cauliflower rice.

Variation Tip: use soy sauce if not getting oyser sauce

Nutritional Information Per Serving:
Calories 78| Fat 7.5g |Sodium 110mg | Carbs 3g | Fiber 1.7g | Sugar 1.2g | Protein 2g

Cajun Shrimp

Prep Time: 10 minutes.
Cook Time: 12 minutes.
Serves: 6

Ingredients:

- 340 g Medium Shrimp, Peeled & Deveined with Tail-On (Cooked Frozen Shrimp)
- 6 lbs Smoked Sausage Rope, Sliced
- 2 lbs Small Potatoes, Halved
- 4 Mini Corn on the Cobs, Quartered
- ¼ Cup White Onion, Diced
- 1/8 Cup Old Bay Seasoning or to Taste
- Olive Oil Spray

Preparation:

1. First, make sure the potatoes are steamed. For this recipe, we used small potatoes cut in half.
2. When the potatoes are ready, mix the remaining ingredients well in a large bowl. (Shrimp can be frozen)
3. Put a piece of foil in your Ninja Foodi, making sure that the air can still circulate.
4. Pour about half of the mixture into the foil to fill the frying basket. Note: We use 4 litter air fryer basket, so we prepare this amount in 2 batches.
5. Once the ingredients are added, sprinkle with a good coat of olive oil spray.
6. Bake 6 minutes at 390 degrees.
7. Open the Ninja Foodi, gently mix the ingredients.
8. Cook for another 6 minutes.

Serving Suggestion: Serve the Cajun Shrimp with quinoa

Variation Tip: use sweet potato intend of potatoes

Nutritional Information Per Serving:

Calories 482| Fat 15.5g |Sodium 2110mg | Carbs 43g | Fiber 4.7g | Sugar 7.2g | Protein 37.7g

Grilled Lobster Tail

Prep Time: 05 minutes.
Cook Time: 05 minutes.
Serves: 2

Ingredients:

- 2-4 Lobster Tail
- 4 Tbsp. Unsalted Butter
- 1 Clove Garlic, Crushed
- 1 Tsp Dried Parsley
- Salt & Pepper to Taste

Preparation:

1. Preheat the Ninja Foodi Grill by setting the grill function to high, grill over high heat for 5 minutes.
2. Starting with kitchen scissors to cut the lobster, cut through the center of the tail until you reach the fins, do not cut the fins.
3. Spread the tail and use your fingers to lift the meat up and close the shell. When you cut, you need to create a butterfly effect on the meat so that it can easily move to the top of the shell. See the video for a tutorial.
4. Melt the butter in a small plate and add the garlic and parsley, mix well.
5. Brush each lobster firmly with the butter mixture using a brush.
6. When preheating is complete, lift the lid of the Ninja Foodi Grill and coat the basket with olive oil spray.
7. Carefully place the lobster tail in the basket.
8. Brush lobster tail evenly with cooking spray.
9. Grill for 5 minutes or until meat has an internal temperature of at least 145 * F.
10. Take out carefully and serve.

Serving Suggestion: Serve the Grilled Lobster Tail with salad

Variation Tip: use coconut oil

Nutritional Information Per Serving:
Calories 450| Fat 25g |Sodium 538mg | Carbs 6g | Fiber 0g | Sugar 0g | Protein 45g

Easy Catfish

Prep Time: 05 minutes.
Cook Time: 20 minutes.
Serves: 4

Ingredients:

- 4 Catfish Fillets or Catfish Nuggets
- ½ Cup Gluten Free Fish Fry
- Olive Oil Cooking Spray

Preparation:

1. Top each fillet of catfish or nugget with an even layer of fried fish.
2. Transfer to the Ninja Foodi and drizzle olive oil on one side of the catfish.
3. Cook for 10 minutes at 390 *F.
4. Gently flip the catfish, brush with spray and cook for another 10 minutes.

Serving Suggestion: Serve the Easy Catfish with ketchup

Variation Tip: use coconut oil

Nutritional Information Per Serving:
Calories 338| Fat 15g |Sodium 314mg | Carbs 5g | Fiber 0g | Sugar 0g | Protein 36g

Fish Tacos

Prep Time: 10 minutes.
Cook Time: 17 minutes.
Serves: 8

Ingredients:

- 4 Tilapia Fillets (or White Fish Fillets)
- 1 Tsp Paprika
- ½ Tsp Salt
- ½ Tsp Pepper
- 8 White Corn Tortillas

Corn Salsa

- 2 Cups Cooked Corn
- 2 Roma Tomatoes, Diced
- ¼ Cup Purple Onion, Diced
- ¼ Cup coriander, Diced
- 1 Lime

Preparation:

1. Coat the Ninja Foodi basket with cooking spray.
2. Place the defrosted fish in the Ninja Foodi basket, top with paprika, salt and pepper.
3. Air Fry for 12 minutes at 360 degrees in the air.
4. While cooking, mix the ingredients for the corn sauce in a small bowl, halve the lime and squeeze the juice over the ingredients for the corn sauce.
5. Once the fish is done cooking, remove it and mince it with a fork.
6. Build each tortilla with fish and top with corn sauce.
7. Place in the deep fryer, placing each tortilla side by side, supporting the sides of the deep fryer.
8. Cover them with cooking spray.
9. Fry for 5 minutes at 360 degrees.
10. Carefully remove with tongs and serve with the Willow of your choice.

Serving Suggestion: Serve the Fish Tacos with salad

Variation Tip: use salmon fish

Nutritional Information Per Serving:
Calories 215| Fat 5g |Sodium 237mg | Carbs 22g | Fiber 3g | Sugar 3g | Protein 25g

Easy Salmon

Prep Time: 05 minutes.
Cook Time: 10 minutes.
Serves: 2

Ingredients:

- 1 lb Salmon (Fillet size of your choice)
- Grapeseed, Avocado, or Coconut Oil Spray
- Garlic and Herb Seasoning

Preparation:

1. Brush the salmon with cooking spray of your choice and season evenly.
2. Let the salmon rest while the Ninja Foodi preheats for about 2-3 minutes.
3. Cook in Air fryer at 400 * F for 10 minutes if cold and 13 minutes if frozen, or until internal temperature reaches 145 * F.
4. Remember to watch the salmon for about 8 minutes as the cooking time may vary depending on the fryer you use.

Serving Suggestion: Serve the Easy Salmon with salad

Variation Tip: use olive oil

Nutritional Information Per Serving:
Calories 378| Fat 25g |Sodium 169mg | Carbs 5g | Fiber 4g | Sugar 0g | Protein 26g

Fish and Grits

Prep Time: 10 minutes.
Cook Time: 30 minutes.
Serves: 2

Ingredients:

- 700 Ml chicken broth
- 240 ml Double cream
- 172g stone ground grits
- 2 Tbsp. butter
- 1 tsp salt
- 2 pieces tilapia fish
- 2 tsp blackened or Cajun seasoning
- vegetable oil in a spray bottle

Preparation:

1. Pour the chicken broth, Double cream, groats, salt and butter into the Ninja Foodi pressure cooker. Stir. Cover with the pressure cooker lid. Make sure the valve is set to "Seal".
2. Cook on high pressure for 8 minutes. After 8 minutes, let Ninja Foodi release naturally for 10 minutes. Press Cancel and release the remaining pressure by turning the valve to "Vent".
3. Meanwhile, season the fish with charred or Cajun seasoning by basting the fish first, then rubbing the seasonings on both sides of the fish.
4. Once all the pressure is released, open the food and stir in the grains. Place a piece of sturdy foil over the grains to cover them. Place the seasoned fish on the foil. Spray again with oil.
5. Close the Air Crisp lid of the Ninja Foodi. Bake at 400 degrees Fahrenheit for 10 minutes or until the fish can easily peel off with a fork.
6. Serve the fish on semolina and enjoy

Serving Suggestion: Serve the Fish and Grits with salad

Variation Tip: use salmon fish

Nutritional Information Per Serving:
Calories 787| Fat 47.5g |Sodium 2510mg | Carbs 72g | Fiber 7g | Sugar 1.1g | Protein 32g

Buffalo Tuna Cakes

Prep Time: 10 minutes.

Cook Time: 10 minutes.

Serves: 4

Ingredients:

- 2 packets (85 g each) Low Sodium Albacore White Tuna in Water
- 60g Breadcrumbs
- 28g Freshly Shredded Parmesan
- 28g Freshly Shredded Cheddar
- 1 large Egg
- 30g Buffalo Sauce
- 1 tsp Paprika
- ½ tsp Garlic Powder
- ½ tsp Onion Powder

Preparation:

1. Combine all the ingredients in a large bowl.
2. Divide the mixture into four pieces of 88 grams. Shape each piece of patty with your hands and place them in a Ninja Foodi Frying Basket.
3. Air fry for 10-12 minutes at 400 ° F or until golden brown.

Serving Suggestion: Serve the Buffalo Tuna Cakes with mayonnaise

Variation Tip: use hot sauce if not getting Buffalo Sauce

Nutritional Information Per Serving:

Calories 178| Fat 7g |Sodium 110mg | Carbs 11g | Fiber 1.7g | Sugar 1.2g | Protein 17g

Crispy Cod

Prep Time: 05 minutes.
Cook Time: 10 minutes.
Serves: 2

Ingredients:

- 1 lb cod fillet
- 1 lemon
- 57 g butter
- 1 tsp salt
- 1 tsp seasoning salt

Preparation:

1. Prepare the ingredients for the cod fillets in the deep fryer. Season the steaks with your favourite seasoning.
2. Brush the Ninja Foodi frying basket with oil. Place the steaks in the basket. Garnish with butter and lemon wedges.
3. Fry the cod at 400 ° C for 10-13 minutes, depending on the size of the fillets. The internal temperature should reach 145 ° F.

Serving Suggestion: Serve the Crispy Cod with sauce

Variation Tip: use tuna

Nutritional Information Per Serving:
Calories 405| Fat 25g |Sodium 1410mg | Carbs 5g | Fiber 2g | Sugar 1g | Protein 41g

Shrimp Risotto

Prep Time: 20 minutes.
Cook Time: 10 minutes.
Serves: 8

Ingredients:

- 2 tablespoons olive oil
- ½ cup diced onions
- 2 teaspoon minced garlic
- 65 ml white wine
- 225g arborio rice
- 700ml chicken broth or chicken stock
- 1 teaspoon salt
- ½ teaspoon black pepper
- 67 g shredded Parmesan cheese
- 1 pound shrimp

Preparation:

1. Start by sautéing the onions in olive oil for a few minutes until they are translucent and tender.
2. Then add the rice and chopped garlic and sauté for a few minutes until the rice is toasted.
3. Add the wine and mix well. You really want to get all those little bits of rice, onion, and garlic sticking to the bottom of the pot. Then add your chicken broth, cheese, salt and black pepper. Mix well. Put the lid in the pressure cooker and set the time to 8 minutes. (High) When the time is up, release the fan by opening the air vent.
4. Mix well after opening the lid.
5. Add the shrimp and press the sear function to sear the Ninja Foodi. Sauté for a few minutes until the shrimp are opaque.
6. Serve, serve and enjoy!

Serving Suggestion: Serve the Shrimp Risotto with salad

Variation Tip: use chicken

Nutritional Information Per Serving:
Calories 265| Fat 5.6g |Sodium 738mg | Carbs 31g | Fiber 1.2g | Sugar 0.2g | Protein 18.2g

Poultry Mains Recipes

Lemon Pesto Whole Chicken

Prep Time: 10 minutes.
Cook Time: 35 minutes.
Serves: 4

Ingredients:

- 3 lb chicken
- ¼ teaspoon salt
- lemon halved
- ¼ teaspoon pepper
- 4 garlic cloves sliced
- 45 g pesto
- 1 red onion quartered
- 118 ML chicken broth or water

Preparation:

1. Rub the chicken down with salt and pepper, squeeze half a lemon over top.
2. Separate the skin from the meat on top of the breast and stuff 3 of the 4 sliced cloves under the skin.
3. Rub the jarred pesto overtop of the chicken skin, underneath with the garlic, and in the cavity.
4. Stuff ¼ of the onion and half the lemon into the cavity of the chicken (you may have to slice it to make it fit).
5. Add the trivet to the Ninja Foodi and place the chicken on top. Surround the chicken with the rest of the onion. Add the liquod (water or broth).
6. Place the lid on top of the Foodi and seal. Turn on high pressure for 22 minutes. Let the pressure come down naturally for 5 minutes. Then release the vent.
7. Remove the lid and close the air fryer lid. Air fry for 12-15 minutes at 400F.
8. Let the chicken rest for 10-15 minutes to let the juices settle.

Serving Suggestion: Serve the Shrimp Risotto with salad

Variation Tip: use chicken

Nutritional Information Per Serving:
Calories 265| Fat 5.6g |Sodium 738mg | Carbs 31g | Fiber 1.2g | Sugar 0.2g | Protein 18.2g

Cream Cheese Shredded Chicken with Bacon

Prep Time: 05 minutes.
Cook Time: 20 minutes.
Serves: 6

Ingredients:

- 2.5 lb chicken breast
- ½ cup water or chicken broth
- 4 oz. cream cheese
- 7 slices bacon
- 1 cup shredded cheese
- half package of ranch dry mix

Preparation:

1. Put the chicken and the broth in a Ninja Foodi saucepan. Sprinkle the ranch on top and add pieces of cream cheese to it. Close and lock the cover. Cook on high pressure for 18 minutes.
2. Meanwhile, brown the bacon in the pan until crispy. Let cool and chop.
3. Once the chicken is cooked, naturally release the pressure for 10 minutes, then quickly release the pressure. Take out the chicken and chop.
4. Stir the broth until smooth (use a silicone spatula or whisk). Add the grated chicken, bacon, chopped green onion and grated cheese. Stir again.

Serving Suggestion: Serve the Cream cheese shredded chicken with bacon with salad

Variation Tip: use turkey

Nutritional Information Per Serving:
Calories 525| Fat 25g |Sodium 714mg | Carbs 2g | Fiber 0g | Sugar 1g | Protein 69g

Apricot Chicken

Prep Time 15 minutes.
Cook Time: 05 minutes.
Serves: 8

Ingredients:

- 2 lbs chicken boneless, skinless breasts, cut into bite size pcs.
- 320 g apricot jam
- 248 g Catalina salad dressing
- 150 ml chicken broth
- 1 onion sliced or diced
- 1 packet French onion soup mix 1 oz.
- 23 g cornflour

Preparation:

1. Add all the ingredients except the corn flour to your pressure cooker and stir to cover everything.
2. Close the lid and the steam valve and activate the high pressure for 4 minutes.
3. Share quickly when you're done.
4. Turn off the pot, then hit the jump. In a separate small bowl, add corn-starch + 4 tbsp. hot liquid from your saucepan. Hit to make it smooth.
5. Pour this corn-starch mixture into your pot as soon as the liquid in your pot starts to bubble. Stir.
6. Stir slowly for 1-2 minutes, it will become a little thicker Then turn off the pot.
7. Let stand for at least 5 minutes to thicken the sauce further. Serve over rice!

Serving Suggestion: Serve the Apricot Chicken with rice

Variation Tip: use turkey

Nutritional Information Per Serving:
Calories 556| Fat 30g |Sodium 733mg | Carbs 43g | Fiber 1.2g | Sugar 28g | Protein 28g

Chicken Breast

Prep Time: 10 minutes.
Cook Time: 10 minutes.
Serves: 4

Ingredients:

- 3 (85 g each) chicken breasts boneless, skinless preferred
- 125 ml water
- 85 g barbecue sauce
- 1 tsp garlic powder
- ½ tsp salt

Preparation:

1. Combine BBQ sauce, garlic powder and salt in a bowl.
2. In a separate bowl, add ½ cup of this barbecue sauce mixture + your water and mix. Instead, at the bottom of your Ninja Foodi.
3. Put down a trivet (the metal your pot comes with works perfectly)
4. Place the chicken breasts on the grill and spread the rest of the barbecue sauce over the meat in your bowl.
5. Close the lid and the steam valve and set the cooking temperature to high pressure for 6 minutes. Naturally, when you are done for 3 minutes, release the pressure. (The time depends on the thickness of your breasts, always check the temperature when you are done to make sure it is in the center)
6. Lift the lid of the pressure cooker and set it aside.
7. Take out the rack with the chicken, set it aside and pour the liquid to the bottom of the pan.
8. Transfer the meat to the frying basket and lower it into the pan. (You can now spread more BBQ sauce if you really want to layer it)

Serving Suggestion: Serve the chicken breast with salad

Variation Tip: use garlic if not available garlic powder

Nutritional Information Per Serving:
Calories 288| Fat 5g |Sodium 1mg | Carbs22g | Fiber 1g | Sugar 18g | Protein 37g

Chicken with Roasted Potatoes

Prep Time: 05 minutes.
Cook Time: 30 minutes.
Serves: 2

Ingredients:

- 10 pounds cubed potatoes
- 2-pound chicken breast
- 3 sticks butter
- 216 g panko bread crumbs
- 1 egg
- 1 tbsp. Italian seasonings
- 60 g shredded Parmesan cheese
- 1 tbsp. garlic powder
- ½ tbsp. salt
- ½ tbsp. pepper

Preparation:

1. Melted butter.
2. Add the garlic powder and Italian spices.
3. Place the potato cubes at the bottom of your Ninja Foodi
4. Pour the butter over the potatoes so that they are well coated.
5. Mix the panko and Parmesan.
6. whip the egg and dip the chicken breast in the egg and then in the panko mixture.
7. Put a coaster on your potatoes.
8. Place your chicken breast on the coaster.
9. Cook for 10 minutes at high manual pressure.
10. Make a quick pitch
11. Remove the Snap-on lid and cook on Air Fry 390 for 15 minutes.
12. If you don't have a ninja, remove the chicken and put it on the grill for 5 minutes.
13. Serve and enjoy!

Serving Suggestion: Serve the Chicken with roasted potatoes with salad

Variation Tip: use sweet potato

Nutritional Information Per Serving:

Calories 805| Fat 30g |Sodium 1038mg | Carbs 96g | Fiber 12g | Sugar 6g | Protein 39g

Teriyaki Chicken, Broccoli & Rice

Prep Time: 05 minutes.
Cook Time: 10 minutes.
Serves: 2

Ingredients:

- 220g long-grain white rice rinsed
- 237ml chicken stock
- 85g frozen mixed vegetables
- 2 teaspoons Sea salt, divided
- 2 teaspoons ground black pepper, divided
- 1 tablespoon Adobo seasoning
- 2 uncooked fresh boneless skinless chicken breasts (8 ounces each)
- 1 head broccoli, cut in 2-inch florets
- 1 tablespoon extra-virgin olive oil
- 72g teriyaki sauce

Preparation:

1. Add the rice, chicken broth, frozen vegetables, 1 teaspoon of salt, 1 teaspoon of pepper and Adobo seasoning to the pot and stir.
2. Place the chicken breasts on a rotating rack and make sure the rack is in the highest position. Place the wire rack in the pot over the rice mixture.
3. Install the pressure cap and make sure the pressure relief valve is in the SEAL position. Select PRINT and set it to high (HI). Set the time to 2 minutes. Select START / STOP to begin.
4. While the chicken and rice cooks, toss the broccoli with the olive oil and remaining salt and pepper in a bowl.
5. When pressure cooking is complete, allow the pressure to naturally release for 10 minutes. After 10 minutes, quickly release any remaining pressure by turning the pressure relief valve to the VENT position. Carefully remove the cap when the device is depressurized.
6. Liberally brush top of chicken breast with teriyaki sauce. Add the broccoli to the chicken on the grill.
7. Close the lid to grill. Select BROIL and set the time to 12 minutes. Select START / STOP to begin.
8. Cooking is complete when the internal temperature of the chicken reaches 165 ° F. Serve the chicken with rice and broccoli.

Serving Suggestion: Serve the Teriyaki Chicken, Broccoli & Rice with salad

Variation Tip: use brown rice

Nutritional Information Per Serving:
Calories 504| Fat 18.2g |Sodium 4438mg | Carbs 36g | Fiber 4.1g | Sugar 7.2g | Protein 47.2g

Easy Turkey-Pesto Meatballs with Penne Pasta

Prep Time: 15 minutes.
Cook Time: 25 minutes.
Serves: 4

Ingredients:

- 1-pound uncooked minced turkey
- ½ cup prepared basil pesto
- ¼ cup panko bread crumbs
- 1 large egg, lightly beaten
- 1 teaspoon Sea salt, divided
- 1 tablespoon extra-virgin olive oil
- 1 onion, peeled, finely chopped
- 3 cloves garlic, peeled, minced
- 2 cups water
- 2 cups prepared marinara sauce
- 2 ½ cups (8 ounces) penne pasta
- ¼ cup chopped fresh basil leaves
- Parmesan cheese for serving

Preparation:

1. Using your hands, combine the turkey, pesto, breadcrumbs, egg and ½ teaspoon of salt in a large bowl. Roll the mixture into meatballs (using only ¼ cup of the mixture per meatball).
2. Put the oil in a saucepan. Select SEAR / SAUTÉ and set the temperature to MD: HI. Select START / STOP to begin. Heat until the oil sparkles. Add the meatballs and fry them until golden brown on all sides, about 10 minutes. Transfer the meatballs to the plate; put aside.
3. Add the onion, garlic and the remaining ½ teaspoon of salt to the pot and cook until just tender, about 3 minutes.
4. Add water, marinara sauce and pasta and reduce heat to MD. Place the golden meatballs in the pasta.
5. Cover the Ninja Foodi with a lid. Do not lock it, but make sure the pressure relief valve is in the VENT position. Simmer until the noodles are tender and the meatballs are cooked through, about 12 to 15 minutes.
6. When you are finished cooking, select START / STOP to deactivate SEAR / SAUTÉ. Season with salt and pepper, sprinkle with basil and Parmesan and serve.

Serving Suggestion: Serve the Turkey-Pesto Meatballs with Penne Pasta with salad

Variation Tip: use chicken

Nutritional Information Per Serving:

Calories 721| Fat 32g |Sodium 1490mg | Carbs 67.3g | Fiber 3.9g | Sugar 7.7g | Protein 49.2g

Coq Au Vin

Prep Time: 20 minutes.
Cook Time: 50 minutes.
Serves: 4

Ingredients:

- 4 strips uncooked bacon, cut in ¼-inch pieces
- 4 cups (8 ounces) cremini or baby bella mushrooms, sliced ¼-inch thick, stems removed
- 1 onion, peeled, diced
- 1 teaspoon Sea salt, divided
- 4 cloves garlic, peeled, divided
- 1 tablespoon tomato paste
- 1 teaspoon fresh thyme leaves, chopped
- 1 tablespoon plain flour
- 1 ½ cups medium-bodied red wine, such as Pinot Noir or Bordeaux
- 1 bay leaf
- 2 pounds uncooked frozen boneless, skinless chicken thighs
- 2 carrots, peeled, cut in ½-inch pieces
- ½ teaspoon ground black pepper
- 1 package (8 ounces) pearl onions, peeled
- 2 ½ tablespoons extra virgin olive oil, divided
- 1 small baguette, cut in ½-inch thick slices (about 8 slices)
- ¼ cup fresh parsley, chopped

Preparation:

1. Select SEAR / SAUTÉ and set it to MD: HI. Place the bacon in the pan. Cook until fat is melted and bacon is crisp, about 8 minutes. Using a skimmer, place the bacon on a paper towel-lined plate and leave the fat in the saucepan.
2. Add the mushrooms, onion and ¼ teaspoon of salt to the pot and cook until the vegetables are lightly browned, about 8 minutes.
3. Add 3 cloves of garlic, the tomato pastes and thyme and cook for 1 minute, then add the flour and cook for another 1 minute. Add the wine and bay leaf, bring to a boil, then select START / STOP to deactivate SEAR / SAUTÉ. Add the chicken and carrots to the pot.
4. Install the pressure cap and make sure the pressure relief valve is in the SEAL position. Select PRESSURE and set HIGH. Set the time to 15 minutes and select START / STOP to start.
5. When the pressure cooker is finished, quickly release the pressure by turning the pressure relief valve to the VENT position. Carefully remove the cap when the device is depressurized.
6. Place the reversible rack in the highest position in the pot. Toss the pearl onions in 1 tablespoon of oil, the remaining 3/4 teaspoons of salt and pepper and place them on the

grill. Close the lid to grill. Select BAKE / ROAST, set the temperature to 375 ° F and the time to 10 minutes. Select START / STOP to begin.
7. After 10 minutes, slide the onion into the pot and remove the grill. Add the onions to the stew.
8. Return the grid to the pot in the highest position above the stew. Brush the baguette slices with the remaining 1 clove of garlic and brush with the remaining 1 ½ tablespoons of oil. Place the slices on the wire rack. Close the lid, select BROIL and set the time to 6 minutes. Select START / STOP to begin.
9. After 3 minutes, flip the baguette slices. Close the lid to continue cooking.
10. When cooking is finished, remove the grill with the bread from the pan, add the cooked bacon and sprinkle with parsley. Serve with toasted baguettes.

Serving Suggestion: Serve the Coq Au Vin with salad

Variation Tip: use beef

Nutritional Information Per Serving:
Calories 651| Fat 29g |Sodium 1038mg | Carbs 23.1g | Fiber 3.2g | Sugar 4.2g | Protein 73g

Chili-Ranch Chicken Wings

Prep Time: 05 minutes.
Cook Time: 20 minutes.
Serves: 4

Ingredients:

- 125 ml water
- 15 g hot pepper sauce
- 28 g unsalted butter, melted
- 30 ml apple cider vinegar
- 2 pounds frozen uncooked chicken wings
- 14 g ranch dressing mix
- ½ teaspoon paprika
- Non-stick cooking spray

Preparation:

1. Start by sautéing the onions in olive oil for a few minutes until they are translucent and tender.
2. Then add the rice and chopped garlic and sauté for a few minutes until the rice is toasted.
3. Add the wine and mix well. You really want to get all those little bits of rice, onion, and garlic sticking to the bottom of the pot. Then add your chicken broth, cheese, salt and black pepper. Mix well. Put the lid in the pressure cooker and set the time to 8 minutes. (High) When the time is up, release the fan by opening the air vent.
4. Mix well after opening the lid.
5. Add the shrimp and press the sear function to sear the Ninja Foodi. Sauté for a few minutes until the shrimp are opaque.
6. Serve, serve and enjoy!

Serving Suggestion: Serve the Shrimp Risotto with salad

Variation Tip: use chicken

Nutritional Information Per Serving:
Calories 500| Fat 35.6g |Sodium 438mg | Carbs 0.4g | Fiber 0.1g | Sugar 0.2g | Protein 38.2g

Chicken Cacciatore with Farfalle

Prep Time: 15 minutes.
Cook Time: 30 minutes.
Serves: 4

Ingredients:

- 30 ml olive oil
- 340 g sliced cremini mushrooms
- 2 red bell peppers, sliced ¼-inch thick, stems and seeds removed
- 1 onion, peeled, thinly sliced
- 2 teaspoons Sea salt, divided
- 2 cloves garlic, peeled, minced
- 1 tablespoon Italian seasoning
- 443 ml petite diced tomatoes
- 125 ml water
- 2 uncooked boneless skinless chicken breasts (170 g each)
- 4 uncooked boneless skinless chicken thighs (85 g each)
- 1 teaspoon ground black pepper
- 226 g farfalle pasta
- ½ cup fresh basil, chopped
- 2 tablespoons capers, drained, chopped
- Parmesan cheese, for serving

Preparation:

1. Select SEAR / SAUTÉ and set it to MD: HI. Select START / STOP to begin. Add olive oil and heat until shiny. Add the mushrooms, peppers, onions and 1 teaspoon of salt to the pot and sauté for about 5 minutes, until the onion is tender and the mushrooms begin to release their liquid. Add the garlic and Italian spices and brown for 1 minute. Add the tomatoes and water and select START / STOP to turn off SEAR / SAUTÉ.
2. Season the chicken with the remaining teaspoon of salt and pepper. Place the chicken over the vegetables.
3. Install the pressure cap and make sure the pressure relief valve is in the SEAL position. Select PRESSURE and set HIGH. Set the time to 15 minutes and select START / STOP to start.
4. When the pressure cooker is finished, quickly release the pressure by turning the pressure relief valve to the VENT position. Carefully remove the cap when the device is depressurized.
5. Transfer the chicken to a cutting board and toss the noodles in the pot. Select SEAR / SAUTÉ and set it to MD: HI. Select START / STOP to begin. Bring to a boil and cook until pasta is al dente, about 10 minutes.
6. Meanwhile, cut the chicken into small pieces. When the pasta is done, add the chicken, basil and capers. Serve with Parmesan.

Serving Suggestion: Serve the Chicken Cacciatore with salad

Variation Tip: use turkey

Nutritional Information Per Serving:
Calories 191| Fat 11.6g |Sodium 938mg | Carbs 7g | Fiber 1.2g | Sugar 3.2g | Protein 16.2

Chicken Piccata Pasta

Prep Time: 15 minutes.
Cook Time: 20 minutes.
Serves: 4

Ingredients:

- 113 g linguini, broken in half
- 473 ml chicken broth, divided
- 1 tablespoon olive oil
- 28 g lemon juice, plus 1 teaspoon zest, divided
- ½ teaspoon Sea salt, plus more for seasoning
- 4 uncooked thin-cut chicken breast fillets (110 g each)
- Ground black pepper, for seasoning
- 43 g plain flour
- 3 tablespoons butter, melted
- 122 g grated Parmesan cheese
- 2 tablespoons capers
- 2 tablespoons fresh parsley, chopped

Preparation:

1. Combine the pasta, 2 cups of broth, oil, 2 tablespoons of lemon juice and salt in a saucepan. Stir to combine.
2. Install the pressure cap and make sure the pressure relief valve is in the SEAL position. Select PRESSURE and set HIGH. Set the time to 5 minutes and select START / STOP to start.
3. When the pressure cooker is finished, quickly release the pressure by turning the pressure relief valve to the VENT position. Carefully remove the cap when the device is depressurized.
4. Salt and pepper the chicken and pour in the flour, shake off the excess. Brush both sides of the chicken with melted butter.
5. Add the Parmesan, capers, remaining chicken broth, remaining lemon juice and lemon zest to the cooked noodles. Place the rotating rack in the highest position in the pot over the pasta and place the chicken on the rack.
6. Close the lid to grill. Select BAKE / ROAST, set the temperature to 375 ° F and the time to 15 minutes. Select START / STOP to begin.
7. Cooking is complete when the chicken is lightly browned. Add the parsley to the pasta, season with salt and pepper and serve with the chicken.

Serving Suggestion: Serve the Shrimp Risotto with salad

Variation Tip: use chicken

Nutritional Information Per Serving:
Calories 189| Fat 15.6g |Sodium 1738mg | Carbs 9.1g | Fiber 0.5g | Sugar 0.7g | Protein 6.2g

French Onion Chicken

Prep Time: 10 minutes.
Cook Time: 30 minutes.
Serves: 4

Ingredients:

- 30 ml olive oil
- 28 g butter, salted
- 2 (119 g) Large chicken breasts or 4 small chicken breasts
- 1 tsp sea salt fine grind
- 1 tsp black pepper
- 1 tsp dried thyme leaves
- 4 cups sliced onions about 2 large onions
- 6 g corn flour
- 300 ml beef stock
- 4 slices Swiss cheese
- 4 slices French Bread

Preparation:

1. Cut the onions into thin slices. If your chicken breast is thick, cut it in half. You want 4 pieces of chicken, about 1 "thick. Combine the spices to make the seasoning mixture.
2. Put the Ninja Foodi on high heat / sauté. Add oil and butter and heat. Sprinkle the seasoning mixture on both sides of the chicken. Use only about half of the seasoning mixture in this step, the other half will be used to flavor the onions.
3. When the oil and butter sizzle, place the chicken breasts in the inner pot and brown for 3-4 minutes. Flip the chicken and add the onions. Brown the chicken for another 3-4 minutes.
4. Remove the chicken breasts and place them on a plate. Add spices to the onions.
5. Lower the lid of the tender crisp and choose to grill for 10 minutes. This will quickly brown the onions. You can also use the brown / sauté function on high power, but you will need to stir the onions every now and then to avoid burning them.
6. Mix 1 tablespoon of corn flour and add 2 tablespoons of beef broth and stir.
7. When the onions are caramelized, apply the sear/sauté over high heat and turn off the pan with the rest of the broth. Make sure to scrape the bottom to reveal the golden bits (honey) as there is tons of flavor in there.
8. Add the cornflour mixture and stir. Return the chicken breasts to the pot and let the liquid boil for 2-3 minutes. Reduce the heat to medium and simmer for about 3 to 5 minutes.
9. Cover each piece of chicken with Swiss cheese. Put the grill in the high position and place the French bread on the grill. Grill for 5 to 10 minutes or until bread is toasted and cheese is melted.
10. Place a chicken breast on a piece of French bread (toasted), garnish with onion and sauce. Enjoy!

Serving Suggestion: Serve the French Onion Chicken with rice

Variation Tip: use turkey or lamb

Nutritional Information Per Serving:
Calories 561| Fat 22g |Sodium 1738mg | Carbs 51g | Fiber 3g | Sugar 12g | Protein 42g

Southwestern Roast Chicken

Prep Time: 10 minutes.
Cook Time: 30 minutes.
Serves: 4

Ingredients:

- 3 lbs whole chicken
- 2 lbs baby potatoes one small bag
- 2 ears of corn cut into 8
- 1 green pepper cut into large cubes
- 1 onion quartered
- 1 head of garlic
- 125 ml chicken broth or water
- coriander optional garnish
- 1 tsp avocado oil I used this spray

Preparation:

1. In the Ninja Foodi pot, add the corn, baby potatoes, 3/4 of the onion and green peppers.
2. Rub the chicken inside and out with the grating mixture.
3. Chop the top of the garlic head and stab it with the knife. Throw it in the cavity of the chicken with ¼ of the remaining onion. Place the chicken over the vegetables.
4. Add the water, put the lid back on, close it and cook over high heat for 22 minutes.
5. Let the chicken come off naturally (this will keep it cooked) for five minutes, then aerate it.
6. Remove the lid from the pressure cooker and quickly spray or brush the avocado oil (this is the one I have).
7. Lower the crisper lid and aerate at 400° F for 10 to 12 minutes.
8. Let the chicken rest for 10 to 20 minutes.

Serving Suggestion: Serve the Roast Chicken with salad

Variation Tip: use sweet potatoes

Nutritional Information Per Serving:
Calories 598| Fat 25g |Sodium 837mg | Carbs 53g | Fiber 7g | Sugar 7g | Protein 38g

Lemon Pepper Chicken Legs

Prep Time: 05 minutes.
Cook Time: 25 minutes.
Serves: 6

Ingredients:

- 8-10 Chicken Legs
- Mrs. Dash Garlic and Herb seasoning - Sprinkled on
- 1 tbsp. Garlic Salt - Sprinkled on
- 1 tbsp. Garlic Powder - Sprinkled on
- Seasoned Pepper - Sprinkled on
- 1 Lemon - washed and dried and half squeezed on the chicken legs and half sliced and laid on legs
- Olive Oil Cooking Spray

Preparation:

1. Place the chicken leg on the Ninja Foodi and lightly spray them with olive oil in cooking spray.
2. Use a sharp knife to cut a slice from the side of the lemon and squeeze the lemon juice directly onto the chicken legs.
3. Sprinkle with Mrs. Pinch, garlic salt, garlic powder and seasoned pepper.
4. Cut the lemon into slices and place the slices on the chicken feet.
5. Press the grill button and cook for 20 to 25 minutes.
6. When the ninja grill beeps, let the chicken feet sit for about 10 minutes without opening the grill cover.
7. After 10 minutes, open the grill lid and, using tongs, place the chicken feet in a bowl and place the lemon wedges around the bowl.

Serving Suggestion: Serve the Lemon Pepper Chicken Legs with salad

Variation Tip: use turkey Leg

Nutritional Information Per Serving:

Calories 1265| Fat 66g |Sodium 738mg | Carbs 3g | Fiber 1.2g | Sugar 0.2g | Protein 118g

Beef, Pork, and Lamb Recipes

Perfect Roast Beef

Prep Time: 05 minutes.
Cook Time: 25 minutes.
Serves: 6

Ingredients:

- 3-pound Top Round Roast
- Rub
- 2 Tbsp. sea salt
- 2 Tbsp pepper course
- 2 ½ tsp onion powder
- 2 ½ tsp garlic powder

Preparation:

1. Let your roast come to room temperature. It takes about 1 hour.
2. Mix the ingredients of the rub and apply liberally to the outside of the meat.
3. Preheat the Ninja Foodi on the grill with the grill low in the inner pot for 10 minutes.
4. Grill the roast beef on the grill over low heat for 25 minutes. Turn off the Ninja Foodi and keep the lid closed for 25 minutes. Follow the directions if the meat is to be cooked at a different temperature.
5. Take out and let stand 10 minutes. Cut into thin slices against the fiber.
6. Serve and enjoy!

Serving Suggestion: Serve the Perfect Roast Beef with salad

Variation Tip: use lamb or pork

Nutritional Information Per Serving:
Calories 386| Fat 66g |Sodium 1738mg | Carbs 3g | Fiber 0.2g | Sugar 0.9g | Protein 58g

Beef & Broccoli

Prep Time: 15 minutes.
Cook Time: 20 minutes.
Serves: 4

Ingredients:

- 118 mL reduced-sodium soy sauce
- 125 mL beef broth
- 45 mL cooking sherry
- 28 g Light brown sugar
- 6 g fresh ginger, peeled, minced
- ¼ teaspoon crushed red pepper
- 1 ½ pounds uncooked skirt steak, sliced against the grain into ½-inch thick slices, fat trimmed
- ½ cup plus 2 tablespoons water, divided
- ½ pond broccoli florets
- 15 g corn-starch
- 4 fresh Spring onions, chopped

Preparation:

1. In a medium bowl, combine soy sauce, broth, sherry, Light brown sugar, ginger and crushed red pepper. Add the steak to the mixture and marinate for 15 minutes.
2. Meanwhile, add ½ cup of water and the Cook & Crisp ™ basket to the pot. Place the broccoli in the basket.
3. Install the pressure cap and make sure the pressure relief valve is in the VENT position. Select STEAM and set the time to 4 minutes. Select START / STOP to begin.
4. When you are finished cooking, carefully remove the Snap-on cover. Remove the basket of broccoli from the pan and set aside. For the water in the pot.
5. Place the steak and marinade in the pot. Install the pressure cap and make sure the pressure relief valve is in the SEAL position. Select PRESSURE and set HIGH. Set the time for 12 minutes. Select START / STOP to begin.
6. When you are finished quick cooking, quickly release the pressure by turning the pressure relief valve to the VENT position. Carefully remove the cap when the device is depressurized.
7. Combine the corn-starch and 2 tablespoons of water in a small bowl and stir until the corn-starch is dissolved. Select SEAR / SAUTÉ and set it to MD: HI. Select START / STOP to begin. Pour the corn-starch mixture into the pot and stir until the sauce thickens.
8. Add broccoli and chives to meat mixture while stirring. Once the broccoli has warmed, select START / STOP for SEAR / SAUTÉ. switch off

Serving Suggestion: Serve the Beef & Broccoli with rice

Variation Tip: use cauliflower also

Nutritional Information Per Serving:
Calories 431| Fat 16g |Sodium 1273mg | Carbs 19g | Fiber 2.3g | Sugar 8.2g | Protein 51.8g

Beef Stroganoff

Prep Time: 05 minutes.
Cook Time: 15 minutes.
Serves: 6

Ingredients:

- 60 mL oil- vegetable or canola
- 1-pound beef stew meat- cut into 1 inch cubes
- 220 g diced white onion
- 1 ½ teaspoon salt
- 1 teaspoon pepper
- 16 g flour
- 473 mL beef broth
- 34 mL Worcestershire sauce
- 34 mL soy sauce
- 18 g minced garlic
- 75 g sliced mushrooms
- 110 g sour cream
- 250 g wide egg noodles

Preparation:

1. Turn on your Ninja Foodi and select the stir-fry function
2. Add the oil and heat for 1 minute.
3. Add the onion and cook until the onion is tender and translucent.
4. Add the meat and season with 1 teaspoon of salt and 1 teaspoon of pepper.
5. Brown the meat on all sides, stirring frequently
6. Add garlic
7. Add Worcestershire sauce and soy sauce
8. Add the mushrooms.
9. Add the flour, making sure to coat the meat and mushrooms.
10. Pour the beef broth and half a teaspoon of salt on top.
11. Close the lid of the pressure cooker and put it on high pressure with the vent on the "gasket" for 10 minutes.
12. When the timer beeps, turn the nozzle to "Prime" and quickly release all pressure.
13. Open the lid and add the egg noodles.
14. Close the lid and press the vent on the "gasket" at high pressure for 5 minutes
15. When the timer rings, naturally release the pressure for 5 minutes.
16. Open the lid and add ½ cup sour cream.
17. Stir and serve!

Serving Suggestion: Serve the Beef Stroganoff with salad

Variation Tip: use low carb soy sauce or coconut amions

Nutritional Information Per Serving:
Calories 499| Fat 26g |Sodium 1380mg | Carbs 39.5g | Fiber 2.6g | Sugar 4.2g | Protein 26.7g

Beef and Mushrooms Stew

Prep Time: 05 minutes.
Cook Time: 25 minutes.
Serves: 6

Ingredients:

- 2lbs Beef Stew Meat, cut in 1" chunks
- 1 pint of mushrooms, cleaned and sliced
- 2 carrots, sliced
- 3 celery stalks, diced
- ½ onion, sliced
- 1lb potatoes, cut in bite-size pieces (see notes)
- 1 beef gravy packet
- 300 mL beef broth, reduced-sodium
- 2 tsp garlic, minced
- 1 ½ tsp Italian Seasoning
- 2 tsp Montreal Steak Seasoning
- Oil for sautéing
- Salt and pepper as desired.

Preparation:

1. Season the meat with salt, pepper, garlic and Italian spices.
2. In Ninja Foodi, press down on the stir-fry and pour enough oil into the pan to sear the meat. (about a tablespoon).
3. Sear the meat to give it some caramel color and flavor. You may need to do this in batches.
4. Put the meat on a plate and add the mushrooms. Let the mushrooms rest for a few moments so that they also take on a small golden color. Add a pinch of salt and pepper to the mushrooms and other vegetables waiting to enter the pot.
5. When the mushrooms are tender, add the carrots, celery and onion to the pot.
6. Sauté these ingredients and stir for a few moments. Add the meat and potatoes.
7. While everything is sautéing in the pot, prepare the package of sauce by mixing it with the broth and also sprinkling with the Montreal Steak Spice.
8. Add to the pot with the meat and vegetables.
9. Add the pressure cooker lid and twist to seal it. Cook on high pressure for 30 minutes. When the cooking time is up, let the steam escape and slowly remove the lid, opening it away from your face.
10. Stir the stew. Turn the pot over to pop again and add your corn flour puree. Stir until thickened. Serve and enjoy!

Serving Suggestion: Serve the Beef and Mushrooms Stew with rice

Variation Tip: use sweet potatoes, corn in stew

Nutritional Information Per Serving:

Calories 461| Fat 16g |Sodium 338mg | Carbs 19.3g | Fiber 3.2g | Sugar 3.2g | Protein 58g

Minced Beef and Rice Casserole

Prep Time: 05 minutes.
Cook Time: 25 minutes.
Serves: 6

Ingredients:

- 1 lb minced Beef (96/4)
- 1-2 Tbsp. Chili Powder, to spice preference
- ½ Tbsp. Garlic Powder
- ½ Tbsp. Onion Powder
- 1 tsp Smoked Paprika
- 1 tsp Sea salt
- ½ tsp Cumin
- ½ tsp Dried Oregano
- 60g Tomato Paste
- 60g Lime Juice
- 480mL Chicken Broth
- 200g bag coriander Lime Right Rice
- 112g Shredded Cheddar Cheese

Preparation:

1. Cook minced beef to a high level with the Foodi stir-fry function. At the end of cooking, add the dry spices. Once the minced beef is fully cooked, add the lime juice and tomato paste and stir.
2. Turn the Foodi over and add the chicken broth and the good rice. Mix well.
3. Close the Foodi and cook for 5 minutes under high pressure with quick release pressure (ventilate immediately).
4. Stir in the minced meat and rice before pouring the grated cheese on top. Use Food's grill function for 3 to 5 minutes until the cheese is melted and bubbly.

Serving Suggestion: Serve the minced Beef and Rice Casserole with salad

Variation Tip: use brown rice

Nutritional Information Per Serving:
Calories 265| Fat 8g |Sodium 738mg | Carbs 13g | Fiber 1.2g | Sugar 0.2g | Protein 28g

Corned Beef and Cabbage

Prep Time: 10 minutes.
Cook Time: 1 hr. 25 minutes.
Serves: 12

Ingredients:

- 4 to 5 pounds' salt beef brisket (with seasoning packet)
- 250 mL chicken stock
- 30 mL balsamic vinegar
- 1 onion, diced
- 7 cloves garlic, peeled
- ½ teaspoon dried thyme leaves
- 3 bay leaves
- 1 ½ pounds gold baby potatoes, scrubbed
- 1 pound carrots, peeled and cut into large pieces
- 1 head green cabbage, cored and cut in wedges

For glaze, if desired:

- 30g light brown sugar, packed
- 125mL water
- 125g Dijon mustard

Preparation:

1. Place the brisket in the pan with the fat side down. Add the sachet of spices, broth, balsamic vinegar, onion, garlic, thyme and bay leaves.
2. Cover the jar with a lid and close the valve.
3. Set the electric pressure cooker to manual or "pressure cooker" for 1 hour 15 minutes or 75 minutes. Press Start / Stop to start the cooking cycle. Once the cycle is complete, naturally release the pressure for 10 minutes before releasing it quickly.
4. Take the breast out of the pan and keep it warm. Also delete the
5. Garlic and bay leaves.
6. Place the potatoes, carrots and cabbage in the pot with the liquid. Cover the jar with a lid and close the valve.
7. Set the electric pressure cooker to manual or "pressure cooker" for 3 minutes. Press Start / Stop to start the cooking cycle. When the cycle is complete, quickly release the pressure.
8. For the frosting: In a small saucepan, heat Light brown sugar and water over medium heat until boiling. Add the mustard and continue cooking until the sauce has reduced, about 2 to 3 minutes.
9. Place the salt beef brisket over the vegetables and pour the frosting over the salt beef. Put the crisp cover back on and set the Air Crisp function to 400 degrees. Cook for 20 minutes.

Serving Suggestion: Serve the salt beef and Cabbage with rice

Variation Tip: use sweet potatoes as well

Nutritional Information Per Serving:
Calories 690| Fat 36g |Sodium 430mg | Carbs 32g | Fiber 5g | Sugar 12g | Protein 58g

Beef Stew & Dumplings

Prep Time: 10minutes.
Cook Time: 30 minutes.
Serves: 4

Ingredients:

- 400g Diced Beef
- 2 Onions Diced
- 400g Carrots Sliced chunky
- 500g Potatoes Peeled and cubed
- 2 tbsp. Cornflour
- 1 tsp Mixed Herbs
- 1 Litre of Beef Stock

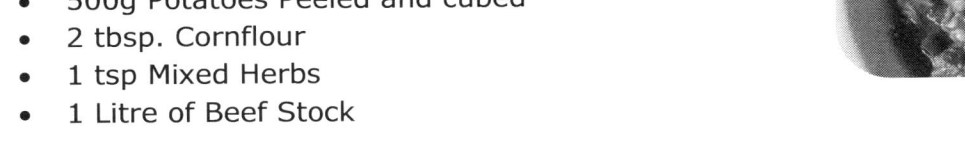

Preparation:

1. Add the onions and beef to the pan and click on Brown / Sauté on high power and you're good to go. Cook until the meat is no longer red on the outside, do not brown. Stir from time to time
2. Add the potatoes and carrots and stir
3. Add the 2 heaped tablespoons of cornmeal, the mixture of herbs, a little salt and pepper. Stir until you can no longer see the dry flour.
4. Stop in action. DO NOT TURN.
5. Cover and cook for 15 minutes over high heat.
6. Mix well, then add the prepared meatballs
7. Bake / roast for 15 minutes at 180 ° C

Serving Suggestion: Serve the Beef Stew & Dumplings with salad

Variation Tip: use diced pork

Nutritional Information Per Serving:
Calories 423| Fat 6.6g |Sodium 1738mg | Carbs 43g | Fiber 5.2g | Sugar 5.2g | Protein 38g

Pulled Pork

Prep Time: 05 minutes.
Cook Time: 2hr. 35 minutes.
Serves: 12

Ingredients:

- 7 lb pork butt
- 245 mL water
- 50 g sugar
- 14 g onion powder
- 14 g seasoned salt
- 14 g smoked paprika
- 10 g chili powder
- 6 g fine grind sea salt
- 3 g celery salt

Preparation:

1. Remove the pork neck at least 30 minutes before cooking. Prepare the seasoning and rub it liberally on the pork. What is left is a dressing that can be used to season meat after cooking or stored for future use.
2. Add 1 cup of water to the inner pot and place the pork fat side up on the wire rack or in a loop and place it in the pot. You want the pork to rise above the liquid. Replace the pressure cap and turn the valve to seal. Cook on high pressure for 90 minutes to make a 7 to 8 pound pork butt. See the tips for cooking tips for small pieces of pork.
3. When the time is up, naturally release the pressure until the pen drops. Open the lid and take out the grill with the pork. Remove the liquid from the pan. I lift it up and store it in the fridge for other uses or to add fat and juice to the meat after pulling it.
4. Return pork to inner pot. I put it straight into the inner pot so that there was enough space between the crispy lid and the top of the pork. Close lid to broil and aerate at 300 ° F / 150 ° C for 1 hour. Check it after 30 minutes to make sure the top isn't getting too dark. Took 1 hour to process and crisp the fat cap each time, but I still love to try.
5. Remove the pork with meat forks or grating forks and place it on a cutting board to cool. When it is cold enough to handle, remove the meat and cut it into pieces of the desired size. The meat should come off very easily. Otherwise, remove the crispy top and pc for an additional 20-30 minutes. If you are using a bone-in stump of pork, remove the bone and discard it.
6. Season the pulled pork with an extra touch or add your favourite barbecue sauce.
7. Serve and enjoy!

Serving Suggestion: Serve the Pulled Pork with barbecue sauce.

Variation Tip: use lamb

Nutritional Information Per Serving:
Calories 327| Fat 16g |Sodium 2201mg | Carbs 6g | Fiber 1g | Sugar 4g | Protein 48g

Sweet and Savory Pork fillet steak

Prep Time: 05 minutes.
Cook Time: 05 minutes.
Serves: 4

Ingredients:

- 1.5-pound pork fillet steak
- 621 mL pork gravy
- 125 mL water
- 6 carrots (cut into 2-3 pieces each)
- 5 red potatoes (large and cut into 5 or 6 pieces each)
- 100 g Light brown sugar
- 56 g butter (salted and cut into 8 pieces)
- 3 sprigs thyme (fresh)
- ¼ teaspoon salt
- ¼ teaspoon pepper

Preparation:

1. Take the pork fillet steak from the package and season lightly with S&P.
2. Pork Tenderloin, Pork, Ninja Foodi Pork, Instant Pork, Carrots, Potatoes
3. Make 1-inch cuts on the pork tenderloin; anything between 6 and 8 will work.
4. Pork Tenderloin, Pork, Ninja Foodi Pork, Instant Pork, Carrots, Potatoes
5. Spread out the grooves a little, then put a piece of butter in each groove.
6. Place the pork tenderloin on the Ninja Foodi.
7. Add the potatoes and carrots around the pork tenderloin.
8. Add the Light brown sugar and try to place it in the center of the pork tenderloin.
9. In a separate bowl, add ½ cup of water to 2 cans of pork sauce and mix well.
10. Pour the pork sauce mixture over the pork tenderloin.
11. Cover with sprigs of fresh thyme.
12. Add the pressure cooker lid.
13. Close and set to high manual power for 5 minutes.
14. When the timer expires, release natural pressure for 10 minutes, then quickly release remaining pressure.
15. Take the net from the Ninja Foodi and save.
16. Open, place on a plate and pour the sauce over the pork tenderloin and vegetables.

Serving Suggestion: Serve the Sweet and Savory Pork Tenderloin with salad

Variation Tip: use your favourite vegetables

Nutritional Information Per Serving:
Calories 695| Fat 20g |Sodium 1238mg | Carbs 88g | Fiber 7g | Sugar 40g | Protein 41g

Pepper Garlic Pork Fillet Steak

Prep Time: 05 minutes.
Cook Time: 10 minutes.
Serves: 6

Ingredients:

- 1 pork fillet steak
- 3 tbsp minced garlic
- 250 mL of beef broth
- 128 g honey
- 15 mL balsamic glaze
- 1 tablespoon ground pepper
- 12g Light brown sugar
- 24 g corn starch
- 60 mL Worcestershire sauce

Preparation:

1. Combine pepper, garlic and Light brown sugar in a small bowl.
2. Rub this mixture on the net and keep it.
3. In your Ninja Foodi casserole, combine 1 cup of beef broth, honey, balsamic glaze and Worcestershire sauce.
4. Whip the contents of Ninja Foodi: use a silicone whisk to avoid scratching the pot
5. Give the net to the Ninja Foodi
6. Cover, close and put in high pressure cooking for 5 minutes, put the valve on "seal"
7. When the timer expires, release natural pressure for 10 minutes, then quickly release remaining pressure. Then remove the net from Ninja Foodi and save
8. Combine the cornflour and the rest of the broth in a glass, shake until completely dissolved.
9. Turn the Ninja Foodi stir-fry for 5 minutes and add the cornflour mixture, beating until thickened
10. Cut the fillet into slices, serve and pour the sauce over it.

Serving Suggestion: Serve the Pepper Garlic Pork Tenderloin with roasted potatoes and carrots

Variation Tip: use garlic powder

Nutritional Information Per Serving:
Calories 265| Fat 1.6g |Sodium 338mg | Carbs 53g | Fiber 0.2g | Sugar 43.2g | Protein 7.8g

Crispy Pork Carnitas

Prep Time: 10 minutes.
Cook Time: 45 minutes.
Serves: 4

Ingredients:

- 2 lbs pork butt cutlet into 2 inch pieces
- 1 tsp Sea salt
- ½ tsp oregano
- ½ tsp cumin
- 1 orange cut in half
- 1 yellow onion peeled and cut in half
- 6 garlic cloves peeled and crushed
- 125 mL chicken broth

Preparation:

1. Place the pork, salt, oregano and cumin seeds in the Ninja Foodi pressure cooker. Toss to make sure the seasonings cover the pork.
2. Take the orange and squeeze the juice over the pork. Put the squeezed orange in the insert along with the onion, garlic cloves and half a cup of chicken broth.
3. Cover the Ninja Foodi with the pressure cooker lid and make sure the valve is fully closed. Put the Ninja Foodi on high pressure and cook for 20 minutes.
4. After the 20-minute timer expires, perform a quick release by switching the valve to vent. Once all the pressure is released, open the lid and remove the orange, onion and garlic cloves.
5. Set Ninja Foodi to Satué and select md: hi. The liquid begins to simmer. Let the liquid boil for about 10-15 minutes until it is reduced.
6. Once most of the liquid is reduced, press Stop on Ninja Foodi, then close the Ninja Foodi Air Crisp lid.
7. Select Broil and set the time to 8 minutes.
8. When you're done, use the delicious crispy meat in tacos, bowls, sandwiches, wraps, and more. Garnish with coriander or one of your favourite toppings.

Serving Suggestion: Serve the Crispy Pork Carnitas with salad

Variation Tip: use lamb

Nutritional Information Per Serving:
Calories 335| Fat 16g |Sodium 838mg | Carbs 8g | Fiber 1g | Sugar 4g | Protein 43g

Herbed Lamb Cutlet

Prep Time: 05 minutes.
Cook Time: 25 minutes.
Serves: 6

Ingredients:

- 2 g rosemary, chopped
- 45 mL extra-virgin olive oil
- 1 garlic clove, minced
- 6(90g) Frenched lamb cutlet
- Ground black pepper
- salt to taste
- 3.2 g chopped fresh mint
- 1 tablespoon agave nectar

Preparation:

1. Place the oil, garlic and rosemary in a bowl. Mix the ingredients together to bind them together.
2. Add lamb, salt and pepper; Cover tightly to marinate and refrigerate for 2-4 hours.
3. Take the Ninja Foodi Grill, place it on your kitchen shelf, and open the lid.
4. Attach the grill grid and close the lid. Press "GRILL" and select the "HIGH" grill function. Set the timer for 12 minutes then press "START / STOP". Ninja Foodi starts preheating.
5. After hearing a beep, open the cover.
6. Place the lamb on the grill rack with herbs. Close the lid and cook for 6 minutes. Now open the top cover, turn the lamb over. Close the lid and cook for another 6 minutes. Cook until the food thermometer reaches 145 ° F.
7. Arrange on a plate and sprinkle with chopped mint and agave nectar. Serve hot.

Serving Suggestion: Serve the lamb cutlet with roasted asparagus, creamy mashed potatoes, beet salad, cucumber salad, and pasta

Variation Tip: use turkey Leg

Nutritional Information Per Serving:
Calories 362| Fat 29.6g |Sodium 328mg | Carbs 2g | Fiber 0.2g | Sugar 0.2g | Protein 22g

Lamb with Mint

Prep Time: 55 minutes.
Cook Time: 60 minutes.
Serves: 6

Ingredients:

- 1.2kg half leg of lamb (raw)
- 3 cloves of garlic (optional - peeled and thinly sliced)
- 25g small bunch fresh mint (finely sliced)
- 20ml rapeseed or vegetable oil
- To taste salt and freshly ground black pepper
- 25g thickening gravy granules

Preparation:

1. Place the lamb on a suitable board (for the meat). If using garlic, prick the meat (about 30 times) with the tip of a sharp knife to make small incisions in the meat
2. Place a slice of garlic in each slit and season the lamb with salt and freshly ground black pepper.
3. Pour 200 ml of cold water into the pan of your Ninja Foodi .
4. Place the lamb in the Cook & Crisp basket and place the basket in the pan (you may need to cut the bone if it is too long for the basket)
5. Install the pressure cap and make sure the relief valve is in the SEAL position. Select PRESSURE and set HIGH. Set the time to 32 minutes. Select START / STOP to begin
6. When pressure cooking is complete, naturally release the pressure for 2 minutes. After 2 minutes, quickly release any remaining pressure by gently moving the pressure release to the WIND position. Remove the cap when the device is depressurized.
7. Brush the lamb with rapeseed / vegetable oil.
8. Close the lid to grill. Select AIR CRISP, set the temperature to 200 ° C and the time to 8 minutes. Select START / STOP to begin. When the cooking process is complete, take the basket out of the pot and cover it loosely with foil on a plate.
9. To make a sauce, add the sauce granules to the pot with the cooking liquid and stir them with a whisk (or a spoon). At this point you can add a little more water, broth, or even a drop of wine if you want. Install the pressure cap and make sure the pressure relief valve is in the SEAL position
10. Select PRESSURE and set it to LOW. Set the time to 3 minutes. Select START / STOP to begin
11. When pressure cooking is complete, quickly release the pressure by setting the pressure release to the VENT position. Carefully remove the cap when the pressure is released.
12. Stir the sauce and adjust the consistency with a little more liquid (water, broth or wine) if it is too thick. Pour the sauce through a sieve into a saucepan or saucepan and add the finely chopped fresh mint.

13. To serve, cut the resting lamb into slices and place it on a warm serving platter. Top with salsa and serve with potatoes (like scallops) and freshly steamed seasonal vegetables.

Serving Suggestion: Serve the LAMB WITH MINT with salad

Variation Tip: use turkey Leg

Nutritional Information Per Serving:
Calories 395| Fat 13.6g |Sodium 0mg | Carbs 3.5g | Fiber 1.2g | Sugar 0.2g | Protein 60g

Roasted Lamb Cutlet

Prep Time: 05 minutes.
Cook Time: 05 minutes.
Serves: 6

Ingredients:

- 16 lamb cutlet rib cutlet OR loin cutlet
- 2 teaspoons Sea salt
- ½ teaspoon black pepper
- ½ teaspoon cayenne pepper or to taste
- 1 teaspoon granulated garlic
- ½ teaspoon onion powder
- 56 g Whole Greek yogurt OR honey

Preparation:

1. Season the lamb with salt, black pepper, cayenne pepper, granulated garlic and onion powder.
2. Brush the lamb with ¼ cup honey OR ¼ cup plain Greek yogurt
3. Grill or roast the lamb for 4 to 7 minutes of Ninja Foodi you have. Turn if needed

Serving Suggestion: Serve the Lemon Pepper Chicken Legs with salad

Variation Tip: use turkey Leg

Nutritional Information Per Serving:
Calories 1265| Fat 66g |Sodium 738mg | Carbs 3g | Fiber 1.2g | Sugar 0.2g | Protein 118g

Dessert Recipes

Chocolate Chip Frying Pan Cookie

Prep Time: 10 minutes.
Cook Time: 25 minutes.
Serves: 6

Ingredients:

- 250 g plain flour
- ½ teaspoon Bicarbonate of soda
- ½ teaspoon Sea salt
- 113 g unsalted butter, softened, plus more for greasing
- 75 g granulated sugar
- 75 g Light brown sugar
- ½ teaspoon vanilla extract
- 1 large egg
- 170 g semi-sweet chocolate chips
- 75 g chopped walnuts, pecans, or almonds, if desired

Preparation:

1. Close the lid to grill. Preheat the unit by selecting BAKE / ROAST, setting the temperature to 325 ° F and setting the time to 5 minutes. Select START / STOP to begin.
2. While the appliance is preheating, combine the flour, baking powder and salt in a bowl.
3. whip butter, sugar and vanilla in a separate bowl until creamy. Add the egg and whip until smooth and fully incorporated.
4. Slowly add the dry ingredients to the egg mixture, about 1/3 at a time. Use a rubber spatula to scrape the sides to work in all of the dry ingredients. Be careful not to over mix, otherwise the cookie will become dense as it bakes.
5. Stir chocolate chips and nuts into cookie dough until evenly distributed.
6. Generously grease the bottom of the Ninja® * multipurpose pan (or an 8-inch pan). Place cookie dough in pan, making sure it is evenly distributed.
7. Once the appliance is preheated, place the tray on the reversible rack and make sure the rack is in the low position. Place the wire rack with the pan in the pan. Close the lid to grill. Select BAKE / ROAST, set the temperature to 325 ° F and the time to 23 minutes. Select START / STOP to begin.
8. Once baking is complete, let the cookie cool for 5 minutes. Then serve hot with the garnishes of your choice.

Serving Suggestion: Serve the Chocolate Chip Frying Pan Cookie with ice cream

Variation Tip: use almond flour if want low carb

Nutritional Information Per Serving:
Calories 596| Fat 29.6g |Sodium 518mg | Carbs 76.3g | Fiber 3.2g | Sugar 36.2g | Protein 9.2g

Apple Pie Filling

Prep Time: 10 minutes.
Cook Time: 10 minutes.
Serves: 8

Ingredients:

- 4 pounds' apples
- 1 orange zest & juice
- 100 g sugar
- 1 tsp vanilla extract

Spice Blend

- 1 tsp cinnamon
- ½ tsp fine grind sea salt
- ¼ tsp nutmeg
- ¼ tsp allspice

Preparation:

1. Grate and squeeze the orange into the inner pot of the Ninja Foodi. Put the sugar in the inner pot.
2. Core, peel and cut the apples into quarters. Put them in the inner pot. Stir several times as you add the apples to prevent them from turning brown.
3. Replace the pressure cap and turn the valve to seal. Set the pressure to high and the time to ZERO minutes. Once the stove has increased its pressure, it will beep to indicate that it is ready. Get instant approval.
4. Stir the apples and cut them into small pieces if necessary. I use my Mix 'N Chop and it works great.
5. Add the vanilla extract. Mix the spices and season to taste. Add more spices and / or sugar as you wish. Let it cool until you are ready to use your cake filling.

Serving Suggestion: Serve the Apple Pie Filling with cookies

Variation Tip: use honey substitute of sugar

Nutritional Information Per Serving:
Calories 175| Fat 1g |Sodium 138mg | Carbs 46g | Fiber 1.2g | Sugar 28g | Protein 1g

Zeppole

Prep Time: 30 minutes.
Cook Time: 25 minutes.
Serves: 12

Ingredients:

- ¼ cup water
- 1 teaspoon active dry yeast
- 25 g sugar plus 1 teaspoon sugar, divided
- 240 g plain flour
- 124 g whole-milk ricotta cheese
- 1 large egg
- Zest of 1 orange
- 1 teaspoon vanilla extract
- 3/4 teaspoon Sea salt
- ¼ teaspoon freshly grated nutmeg
- 185 g unsalted butter, softened, divided
- Confectioners' sugar, for dusting

Preparation:

1. Heat the water to 110 ° F, then add the yeast and 1 teaspoon of sugar to the bowl of a food processor and let stand for about 5 minutes until the mixture becomes frothy.
2. Add the flour, ricotta, egg, orange zest, vanilla, salt, nutmeg and the remaining 2 tablespoons of sugar and place the bowl in the food processor with a dough hook. Mix on low speed until a dough form.
3. Gradually add ½ cup of the butter, one tablespoon at a time, occasionally stopping the mixer to scrape the sides of the bowl. Increase speed to medium and whip until dough is cohesive, smooth and shiny, about 4 minutes. If necessary, remove the dough from the hook and along the sides of the bowl. Remove the bowl from the blender, cover with Cling film and let rise at room temperature for 2 hours.
4. Place the dough on a lightly floured surface and shape into a smooth ball. Divide into 12 equal portions and roll into firm balls. Place on a Baking tray and let stand, covered, 30 minutes at room temperature.
5. Close the crispy lid after 30 minutes. Preheat the unit by selecting AIR CRISP, setting the temperature to 360 ° F and setting the time to 3 minutes. Select START / STOP to begin.
6. Melt the remaining ¼ cup of butter. Brush half the balls with melted butter and place them in the Cook & Crisp ™ basket. Save unused butter.
7. Once the appliance is preheated, place the basket in the pan. Close the cover. Select AIR CRISP, set the temperature to 360 ° F and the time to 12 minutes. Select START / STOP to begin.
8. Cooking is complete when the zeppoles are golden brown. Remove from the basket, brush again with melted butter and sprinkle with icing sugar.
9. Repeat steps 6 to 8 with the remaining meatballs. Serve hot.

Serving Suggestion: Serve the Zeppole with chocolate sauce

Variation Tip: use coconut flour

Nutritional Information Per Serving:
Calories 265| Fat 16g |Sodium 238mg | Carbs 20.3g | Fiber 1.1g | Sugar 5.2g | Protein 4g

Brownies

Prep Time: 05 minutes.
Cook Time: 4 hr.
Serves: 16

Ingredients:

- 114 grams' butter, salted
- 113 grams' dark chocolate chips
- 113 grams' milk chocolate chips
- 200 grams' sugar
- 2 Tbsp. Rapeseed oil
- 1 Tbsp. vanilla extract
- 3 large eggs slightly beaten
- 29 grams' cocoa powder unsweetened
- 156 grams flour all purpose

Preparation:

1. Add the butter to the Ninja Foodi and set it on high sear/sauté. Add the chocolate chips to the side of the butter when it's about half melted. Stir and melt the chips until they are about 75% melted, then turn off the Foodi. Continue stirring to allow the chocolate to cool.
2. Stir in the sugar and oil until well combined.
3. While whisking the brownie batter, lightly beat the eggs and slowly pour them into the batter. Continually stir until the eggs are fully mixed. Pour in the vanilla extract and whisk to combine.
4. Stir in the unsweetened cocoa powder after sifting it in. Sift in 13 tablespoons of flour at a time, stirring after each addition.
5. Turn the valve to VENT and close the pressure lid. Select the low-heat setting.
6. You can scoop out the brownies if you want warm and gooey or put the Tender Crisp lid down for 8-10 minutes on Air Crisp at 375° to get that flaky top. Cool and serve.

Serving Suggestion: Serve the Brownies with ice cream

Variation Tip: use almond flour

Nutritional Information Per Serving:
Calories 245| Fat 14g |Sodium 738mg | Carbs 23g | Fiber 2g | Sugar 12g | Protein 3g

Lemon Basil Scones

Prep Time: 15 minutes.
Cook Time: 25 minutes.
Serves: 8

Ingredients:

- 250 grams Flour all purpose
- 1 Tbsp baking powder
- 100 grams sugar
- ½ tsp sea salt
- 113 grams butter salted
- 2 lemons zested
- 1 tsp lemon extract or vanilla
- 1 large egg
- 119 grams Double cream plus 1 Tbsp for basting
- 6 grams chopped basil
- 1 Tbsp Demerara Sugar

Preparation:

1. Grate cold butter with a grater and place it in the freezer for 15-30 minutes.
2. Sift the flour into a large mixing bowl. Add the baking powder, sugar, salt. Mix
3. In a small bowl, add 1 egg, ½ cup of whipped cream, 1 teaspoon of lemon extract and the zest of 2 lemons.
4. Use a pastry cutter or two forks to cut the frozen butter into the flour mixture until it looks like a crumb.
5. Pour in the liquid mixture and stir. Don't stir too much.
6. Add the chopped basil and mix, do not stir too much.
7. Pour the mixture onto a cutting board. He will be loose at this point. Press down on the dough, then fold it towards you, working through the loose flour mixture. Flip and repeat until a smooth dough form. If your dough is too sticky, you can add a little more flour. Don't overwork the dough, we don't want the butter to melt.
8. When all of the loose dough is incorporated, the dough should be smooth but not sticky. If the dough sticks to your hands, add a tablespoon of flour at a time and fold until the dough is no longer sticky.
9. Make a 7 inch slice. You can use a 7 inch pizza pan or a removable pan covered with Cling film, or just watch. Cut into 8 quarters and place on a Baking tray lined with baking paper. Refrigerate for 15 minutes to 1 hour.
10. Preheat the Ninja Foodi at 350 ° for 10 minutes. Take the rolls out of the refrigerator, brush them with cream, sprinkle with demerara sugar and place them in a lightly buttered 8-inch cake pan. Bake in Ninja Foodi oven on low heat for 15 minutes.
11. After 15 minutes, run a cake tester along the sides of the slices. Lower the bake / broil temperature to 325 ° F and continue cooking for an additional 3 to 7 minutes. If you find the top is browning too much and the inside is still damp, turn the heat down to 300 ° F.

12. Remove, run a cake tester around all edges and between each loaf. Let cool on a wire rack for at least 30 minutes. The longer you let them cool, the easier it will be to get them out of the pan. Run a cake tester along the edges and between each loaf. Serve and enjoy!

Serving Suggestion: Serve the Lemon Basil Scones with chocolate coffee

Variation Tip: use coconut flour

Nutritional Information Per Serving:
Calories 365| Fat 66g |Sodium 238mg | Carbs 43g | Fiber 2g | Sugar 12g | Protein 5g

Courgette Bread

Prep Time: 10 minutes.
Cook Time: 35 minutes.
Serves: 12

Ingredients:

- 2 large eggs
- 150 grams' sugar
- 1 tsp vanilla
- 78.86 mL vegetable oil or canola
- 186 grams' Courgette grated or 2 small Courgette
- 0.5 tsp sea salt fine grind
- 0.75 tsp cloves ground
- 0.5 Tbsp cinnamon ground
- 125 grams flour
- 2 tsp baking powder

Preparation:

1. Butter and flour your cake pan
2. Preheat the Ninja Foodi to 275 ° F / 135 ° C for 10 minutes.
3. Grate the Courgette with the fine side of a box grater or other grater. Squeeze the liquid from the Courgette.
4. Combine 2 eggs, 1 cup of sugar, 1 teaspoon of vanilla and ⅓ cup of vegetable oil in a medium bowl and mix
5. Add the cinnamon, cloves, salt, flour and baking powder to the wet ingredients and stir until all of the flour is gone.
6. Stir in the Courgette and pour the dough into the prepared bread pan
7. Place the bread pan on the rack in the lower position in the Ninja Foodi inner pot and set bake / broil to 275 ° F and bake for 35-40 minutes. View Recipe Notes
8. Check readiness with a thermometer, temperature should be around 200 ° F / 93 ° C. Remove and let cool on wire rack for 30-60 minutes before serving

Serving Suggestion: Serve the Courgette Bread with coffee

Variation Tip: use squash if not want to use Courgette

Nutritional Information Per Serving:
Calories 265| Fat 66g |Sodium 138mg | Carbs 23g | Fiber 1g | Sugar 12g | Protein 8g

Rice Pudding

Prep Time: 05 minutes.
Cook Time: 15 minutes.
Serves: 10

Ingredients:

- 185 grams White Rice
- 354 grams Jasmine Tea brewed
- ½ tsp Cinnamon
- ¼ tsp Nutmeg
- 1/8 tsp sea salt
- 2 tsp Cardamom
- 396.89 grams Sweetened Condensed Milk
- 72.5 grams' raisins I used golden
- 1 egg lightly beaten
- 121 grams Single cream or heavy whipping cream
- 1 tsp vanilla extract

Preparation:

1. Prepare 1 ½ cup of jasmine tea. Please see the post for different ways of brewing tea. Pour 1½ cups of jasmine tea into the Ninja Foodi's inner pot.
2. Add 1 cup of rinsed jasmine or white rice to the inner pot.
3. Add the spices; ½ teaspoon of cinnamon, ¼ teaspoon of nutmeg, teaspoon of sea salt and 2 teaspoons of cardamom.
4. Stir and close the lid. Make sure the valve is tight. Put at high pressure for 5 minutes. Let Ninja Foodi naturally deflate for 5 minutes, then manually release the remaining pressure. Remove the cap.
5. Turn the sauce over high heat and add the sweetened condensed milk, 1 lightly beaten egg and ½ cup of golden raisins. Stir frequently for about 5 minutes.
6. Add ¼ to ½ cup of heavy, Single cream or Double cream until the jasmine pudding is the desired consistency. Turn off the Ninja Foodi.
7. Add the vanilla extract, mix. Serve and enjoy!

Serving Suggestion: Serve the Rice Pudding with some snacks

Variation Tip: use brown rice

Nutritional Information Per Serving:
Calories 241| Fat 6g |Sodium 98mg | Carbs 43g | Fiber 1g | Sugar 22g | Protein 8g

Pound Cake

Prep Time: 10 minutes.
Cook Time: 25 minutes.
Serves: 12

Ingredients:

- 227 grams butter
- 227 grams sugar
- 4 large eggs room temp
- 1 Tbsp. Vanilla Extract
- 226.8 grams flour
- 1 orange zest only
- 1 Tbsp. butter for greasing pan
- 3 Tbsp. Demerara Sugar

Preparation:

1. Combine butter and sugar with a stand mixer and whip with the spatula until light and fluffy. Scratch the pages every few minutes.
2. Add one egg at a time and whip over low heat until just incorporated. Repeat with the remaining 3 eggs.
3. Add 1 tablespoon of vanilla extract and mix to work only.
4. Slowly add the flour and mix in a stand mixer. Mix over low heat until all the flour is incorporated, without over-mixing.
5. Add the zest of an orange and mix.
6. Butter a 7 "pan in the pan. Add 3 tablespoons of demerara sugar to the pan and move it to stick to the sides. Try to avoid the center.
7. Put 2 cups of water in the inner pot of the Ninja Foodi. Cover the cake with foil and cover a little. Put the stand in the lower position of the Ninja Foodi. Put the pressure on high for 25 minutes. Make sure the black valve is in the sealing position. When the time is up, let it loosen naturally for 20 minutes *.
8. When natural release ends, manually release all pressure. There may not be and the red pin is already in. Place on a cooling shelf and let cool for 5 minutes.
9. Turn the cake over to the cooling rack and gently place the cake on the rack over low heat. Take the cake back to Ninja Foodi. Set Bake / Broil to 400 ° F and bake for 5 to 10 minutes or until top is golden brown.
10. Take out and let cool on the grill for about an hour. Serve and enjoy!

Serving Suggestion: Serve the Pound Cake with tea

Variation Tip: use lemon zest

Nutritional Information Per Serving:
Calories 365| Fat 16g |Sodium 170mg | Carbs 36g | Fiber 1.2g | Sugar 22g | Protein 4g

Pumpkin Pie

Prep Time: 05 minutes.
Cook Time: 10 minutes.
Serves: 8

Ingredients:

- 3 large eggs
- 67 grams sugar
- 123 grams pumpkin puree
- 2 Tbsp. vanilla extract
- 2 tsp pumpkin pie spice
- 182 grams Single cream
- 238 grams heavy whipping cream

Preparation:

1. Combine eggs and sugar in a medium mixing bowl. whip until just combined.
2. Add tinned pumpkin and pumpkin pie seasoning. whip until just combined.
3. Add the vanilla extract, Single cream, and heavy whipped cream. whip until just combined. Mix in 8 Mason jars (4 ounces).
4. Place the lids on the mason jars and tighten by hand. Put 1 cup of water in the inner pot of the Ninja Foodi.
5. Put the glasses in the basket in two layers. Replace the pressure cap and turn the black valve to seal. Cook on high pressure for 7 minutes. Allow it to deflate naturally for 7 minutes, then manually release the remaining pressure.
6. Take the glasses out of the basket and let them sit for about 15 minutes. Then place in the refrigerator for 4 hours.
7. Top with whipped cream and pumpkin pie spice. Serve and enjoy!

Serving Suggestion: Serve the pumpkin pie with sandwich

Variation Tip: use coconut cream

Nutritional Information Per Serving:
Calories 211| Fat 16g |Sodium 58mg | Carbs 13g | Fiber 1g | Sugar 9g | Protein 8g

Eggnog

Prep Time: 10 minutes.
Cook Time: 30 minutes.
Serves: 8

Ingredients:

- 10 large eggs
- 100 grams sugar
- 484 grams half & half
- 1 tsp ground cinnamon
- 1 tsp ground nutmeg
- ½ tsp ground cloves
- 2 tsp vanilla extract
- 238 grams heavy whipping cream

Preparation:

1. Break the eggs into Ninja Foodi's inner pot, add the sugar and Single cream. Bring the Ninja Foodi to a boil / stir
2. Use a silicone whisk to whip the eggs and Single cream. If you don't have a silicone broom, whip the eggs before adding them to the inner pot.
3. Let the saucepan heat the mixture to 150 ° F / 66 ° C. This usually takes about 25 minutes and you will need to whip or stir frequently to keep the egg mixture from boiling to the bottom.
4. If your mixture doesn't reach 150 ° F / 66 ° C after 20 minutes, increase the heat to low to medium, stirring constantly. Bring the temperature to 150-155 ° F / 66-68 ° F, then lower the temperature to a minimum and hold the temperature at 150 ° F / 66 ° F for 5 minutes. If your mix is above 160 ° F / 71 ° FF starts, remove the inner pot to prevent the temperature from rising and place the eggs inside. Stir constantly.
5. Add the seasonings, vanilla extract and whipped cream. Whisk to combine. Chill for at least 4 hours. Serve and enjoy.

Serving Suggestion: Serve Eggnog with Doughnut Muffins.

Variation Tip: use honey

Nutritional Information Per Serving:

Calories 365| Fat 26g |Sodium 138mg | Carbs 17g | Fiber 1g | Sugar 12g | Protein 11g

Triple Chocolate Cheesecake

Prep Time: 30 minutes.
Cook Time: 30 minutes.
Serves: 10
Ingredients:

Cheesecake Crust

- 170 grams chocolate animal crackers
- 7 Tbsp. butter salted or unsalted

Chocolate Cheesecake Filling

- 120 grams dark chocolate chips Ghirardelli preferred
- 227 grams cream cheese room temperature
- 100 grams white sugar
- 1 tsp instant espresso powder optional
- ½ tsp fine grind sea salt
- 1 tsp vanilla extract
- 2 large eggs room temperature

Ganache & Topping

- 177.44 mL heavy whipping cream
- 135 grams dark chocolate chips Ghirardelli preferred
- 90 grams mini chocolate chips any kind is fine

Preparation:

Cheesecake Crust

1. Melt the butter in the microwave or on the stove. Using a food processor or by hand, mix the 3 cups of animal chocolate cookies until well blended.
2. Place animal chocolate cookies in a medium bowl and add butter. Stir to combine. The mixture should be moist and should be able to fit in your hand when squeezed.
3. If you want to put your cheesecake on a platter, you can place a round of baking paper at the bottom of the pan before pressing on the crust. It will make things easier.
4. Squeeze cookie mixture onto sides and bottom of 7¼ "pull-out pan. If you are using a larger pan, you may need to mix in a little more cookie mixture and butter to cover the entire pan. Biscuits almost on the side of the removable pan in this recipe, but you should go up at least ¾ on the sides.
5. Place the removable pan with the crust on the Ninja Foodi rack in the low position and place it in the inner pot, close the lid to broil and bake at 325 ° F / 160 ° C for 5 minutes. No preheating required. Stir and cool

Cheesecake filling

6. Melt chocolate in double boiler or microwave and stir until smooth. Put aside.
7. Place sugar and cream cheese in a medium mixing bowl and whip with a stand mixer or hand mixer on low or medium speed until the sugar is incorporated. with cream cheese.
8. Add melted chocolate, espresso powder (if using) and whip on medium speed until chocolate is incorporated. Add salt and vanilla extract and whip on medium speed until just incorporated. Do not mix the dough too much or you could introduce too much air, which could crack it on your cheesecake.
9. Add the eggs at a time and whip on medium speed until just incorporated. Add the second egg and whip on medium speed until just incorporated.

Cook the cheesecake under pressure

10. Pour the filling into the cooled crust and cover with foil or these silicone toppings. Makes 1 cup of water in the inner pot. Place the covered cheesecake pan in the lower position on the rack and close the lid. Turn the valve to seal. Put the pressure on high for 25 minutes. When the time is up, allow the pot to loosen naturally for 10 minutes.
11. Wipe off any excess water from the top of the lid with a paper towel and remove the lid. Refrigerate the whole cheesecake on the counter for about 30 minutes. Cover again and refrigerate for at least 4 hours. 8 hours or overnight will work best.

Chocolate ganache and coverage

12. ¾ Place a cup of chocolate chips in a medium size mixing bowl.
13. Heat the cream at the bottom of the inner pot or small pot on the stove. You don't want to boil the cream, you want to simmer it where there are bubbles.
14. Pour the hot cream over the chocolate chips and let stand for 5 minutes.
15. whip cream and melted chocolate until you obtain a shiny, pourable chocolate.
16. Remove the sides of the cheesecake and place the cheesecake on the platter or plate. Pour the ganache in the center of the cheesecake and let it run over the outer edges. Flatten the ganache with the back of a large spoon, making sure it spreads to the edges.
17. Spread the mini chocolate chips over the ganache and refrigerate the cheesecake for about 30 minutes to allow the ganache to set completely.
18. Slice, serve and enjoy!

Serving Suggestion: Serve the Triple Chocolate Cheesecake with chips

Variation Tip: use Light brown sugar

Nutritional Information Per Serving:
Calories 1265| Fat 66g |Sodium 738mg | Carbs 3g | Fiber 1.2g | Sugar 0.2g | Protein 118g

4 Weeks Meal Plan

1st week Meal Plan

Day	Breakfast	Lunch	Snack	Dinner	Dessert
1	Chocolate Oatmeal	Cajun Shrimp	Buffalo Cauliflower	Baked Beans	Eggnog
2	Cinnamon Rolls	Chicken Breast	Easy Chickpeas	Beef & Broccoli	Brownies
3	Ninja Foodi Quiche	Pulled Pork	Easy Chickpeas	French Onion Chicken	Pound Cake
4	Breakfast Casserole	Beef Stew & Dumplings	Ninja Foodi Pizza Rolls	Southwestern Roast Chicken	Zeppole
5	Hash Browns	Minestrone Soup	Ninja Foodi tofu	Easy Salmon	Triple Chocolate Cheesecake
6	Fried Eggs	Quinoa with Vegetables	Ninja Foodi Corn Dog Bites	Fish Tacos	Rice Pudding
7	Breakfast Muffins	Shrimp Risotto	Buffalo Wings	FRIED RICE	Courgette Bread

2nd week Meal Plan

Day	Breakfast	Lunch	Snack	Dinner	Dessert
1	Hash Browns	Roasted lamb chops	French Fries	Crispy Pork Carnitas	Pumpkin Pie
2	Cinnamon Rolls	Vegan Chili	Ninja Foodi Eggplant Chips	Grilled Shrimp Foil Packs	Rice Pudding
3	Breakfast Muffins	Easy Salmon	Ninja Foodi Kale Chips	Lemon Pepper Chicken Legs	Triple Chocolate Cheesecake
4	Breakfast Casserole	Beef Stew & Dumplings	Buffalo Cauliflower	Apricot Chicken	Courgette Bread
5	Ninja Foodi Quiche	Coq Au Vin	Ninja Foodi Roasted Potatoes	Shrimp Risotto	Brownies
6	Fried Eggs	Veggie Pot Pie	Ninja Foodi Kale Chips	Minestrone Soup	Zeppole
7	Chocolate Oatmeal	Herbed Salmon	Ninja Foodi tofu	Herbed Lamb cutlet	Pound Cake

3rd week Meal Plan

Day	Breakfast	Lunch	Snack	Dinner	Dessert
1	Breakfast Muffins	Fish Tacos	Buffalo Wings	Baked Beans	Lemon Basil Scones
2	Ninja Foodi Quiche	Lemon Pesto Whole Chicken	Ninja Foodi Pizza Rolls	Grilled Lobster Tail	Pumpkin Pie
3	Hash Browns	Fish and Grits	Ninja Foodi Eggplant Chips	Teriyaki Chicken, Broccoli & Rice	Courgette Bread
4	Cinnamon Rolls	Spinach and Chickpea Stew	Ninja Foodi Coconut Shrimp	Beef & Broccoli	Brownies
5	Fried Eggs	Chicken Piccata Pasta	Buffalo Cauliflower	Roasted lamb cutlet	Pound Cake
6	Chocolate Oatmeal	Pulled Pork	Ninja Foodi Kale Chips	Cajun Shrimp	Zeppole
7	Fried Eggs	Pepper Garlic Pork Tenderloin	Easy Chickpeas	Herbed Lamb cutlet	Apple Pie Filling

4th week Meal Plan

Day	Breakfast	Lunch	Snack	Dinner	Dessert
1	Fried Eggs	Sweet and Savory Pork Tenderloin	Buffalo Wings	Chili-Ranch Chicken Wings	Rice Pudding
2	Hash Browns	Chicken Cacciatore with Farfalle	Ninja Foodi Kale Chips	Crispy Cod	Lemon Basil Scones
3	Cinnamon Rolls	Beef Stroganoff	Ninja Foodi Coconut Shrimp	Falafel	Zeppole
4	Breakfast Muffins	Apricot Chicken	Ninja Foodi Pizza Rolls	Crispy Pork Carnitas	Apple Pie Filling
5	Breakfast Casserole	Vegan Chili	Easy Chickpeas	Chicken Breast	Chocolate Chip Frying Pan Cookie
6	Ninja Foodi Quiche	Lemon Pesto Whole Chicken	Buffalo Cauliflower	Buffalo Tuna Cakes	Courgette Bread
7	Chocolate Oatmeal	Easy Catfish	French Fries	STIR-FRIED BOK CHOY	Triple Chocolate Cheesecake

Conclusion

THE BENEFIT OF A NINJA FOODI:

1. Combines two often used devices in one. Obviously, for me, the air fryer and pressure cooker are two devices I use often.
2. Don't have to move hot food around. Having an air fryer and a pressure cooker in one device means that you don't have to move hot food from a pressure cooker to an air fryer, so it's safer.
3. Less storage than 2 devices. This is a large device, but since it's two devices in one, even with its large size it still takes up less room than two devices would. This would also be convenient for small kitchens, dorm rooms, or for those who travel a lot.
4. One less thing to clean. Plus, it's one less device you have to clean at the end of the night, which is a big plus for me. Efficiency is key.
5. Bake/Roast function. So, in addition to serving as a pressure cooker, an air fryer, a steamer, AND a slow cooker, this device is also a small portable oven. This could make the device quite a kitchen powerhouse device if you used all the features of the Ninja Foodi.

Printed in Great Britain
by Amazon